# 2nd Workshop on Continuous Vector Space Models and Their Compositionality

# (CVSC 2014)

**Held at the 14th Conference of the European Chapter of the Association for Computational Linguistics**

## Gothenburg, Sweden
## 26 - 30 April 2014

**ISBN: 978-1-63266-410-5**

**Printed from e-media with permission by:**

Curran Associates, Inc.
57 Morehouse Lane
Red Hook, NY 12571

**Some format issues inherent in the e-media version may also appear in this print version.**



Printed by Curran Associates, Inc. (2014)

For permission requests, please contact the Association for Computational Linguistics at the address below.

Association for Computational Linguistics
209 N. Eighth Street
Stroudsburg, Pennsylvania 18360

Phone: 1-570-476-8006
Fax: 1-570-476-0860

acl@aclweb.org

**Additional copies of this publication are available from:**

Curran Associates, Inc.
57 Morehouse Lane
Red Hook, NY 12571 USA
Phone: 845-758-0400
Fax: 845-758-2634
Email: curran@proceedings.com
Web: www.proceedings.com

# Introduction

Welcome to the 2nd Workshop on Continuous Vector Space Models and their Compositionality.

The first workshop on Continuous Vector Space Models and their Compositionality attempted to bridge the communities working on various kinds of semantics models relying on continuous representations of textual data.

This year, we continued in this direction and also expended our call for papers to work that asks theoretical and conceptual questions too, such as: Should phrase representations and word representations be of the same sort? Could different linguistic levels require different modelling approaches? Should word representations be task-specific, or should they be general? And many others.

This year's list of topics also included neural networks, distributional semantic models, language modeling for automatic speech recognition, statistical machine translation and information retrieval, the role of syntax in compositional models, the integration of distributional representations with other models, and more.

In brief, we aimed to continue the ongoing effort to address some of these points, either by theoretical reasoning, or through example via demonstrating interesting properties of new or existing distributional models of semantics.

We received 7 submissions, of which we accepted 5 for the final proceedings after a rigorous reviewing process. The workshop program also features the presentation of 3 invited speakers: Ivan Titov (University of Amsterdam), Phil Blunsom (University of Oxford) and Geoffrey Zweig (Microsoft Research).

We hope to gather formal semanticists, computational linguists, machine learning researchers and computational neuroscientists to tackle the fascinating problems behind continuous vector space models.

## Organizers

Alexandre Allauzen, LIMSI-CNRS/Université Paris-Sud

Raffaella Bernardi, University of Trento

Edward Grefenstette, University of Oxford

Hugo Larochelle, Université de Sherbrooke

Christopher Manning, Stanford University

Scott Wen-tau Yih, Microsoft Research

## Program Committee

Nicholas Asher, IRIT-Toulouse

Marco Baroni, University of Trento

Yoshua Bengio, Université de Montréal

Gemma Boleda, University of Texas

Antoine Bordes, Université Technologique de Compiègne

Johan Bos, University of Groningen

Léon Bottou, Microsoft Research

Xavier Carreras, Universitat Politècnica de Catalunya

Lucas Champollion, New-York University

Stephen Clark, University of Cambridge

Shay Cohen, Columbia University

Ronan Collobert, IDIAP Research Institute

Ido Dagan, Bar Ilan University

Maarten de Rijke, University of Amsterdam

Pino Di Fabbrizio, Amazon

Georgiana Dinu, University of Trento

Kevin Duh, Nara Institute of Science and Technology

Dean Foster, University of Pennsylvania

Alessandro Lenci, University of Pisa

Louise McNally, Universitat Pompeu Fabra

Fabio Massimo Zanzotto, Università degli Studi di Roma

Mirella Lapata, University of Edinburgh

Andriy Mnih, Gatsby Computational Neuroscience Unit

Larry Moss, Indiana University

Diarmuid Ó Seaghdha, University of Cambridge

Sebastian Pado, Universität Stuttgart

Martha Palmer, University of Colorado

John Platt, Microsoft Research

Mehrnoosh Sadrzadeh, University of London

Holger Schwenk, Université du Maine

Chung-chieh Shan, Indiana University

Mark Steedman, University of Edinburgh

Peter Turney, NRC

Jason Weston, Google

Guillaume Wisniewski, LIMSI-CNRS/Université Paris-Sud

# Table of Contents

# Workshop Program

**Sunday, April 27, 2014**

| | |
|---|---|
| 9:30–9:40 | Opening Remarks |
| 9:40–10:30 | Invited Talk by Ivan Titov |
| 10:30–11:00 | Coffee Break |
| 11:00–11:20 | *Post-hoc Manipulations of Vector Space Models with Application to Semantic Role Labeling*<br>Jenna Kanerva and Filip Ginter |
| 11:20–11:40 | *Distributional Composition using Higher-Order Dependency Vectors*<br>Julie Weeds, David Weir and Jeremy Reffin |
| 11:40–12:00 | *A Systematic Study of Semantic Vector Space Model Parameters*<br>Douwe Kiela and Stephen Clark |
| 12:00–14:00 | Lunch Break |
| 14:00–14:50 | Invited Talk by Geoffrey Zweig |
| 14:50–15:10 | *Extractive Summarization using Continuous Vector Space Models*<br>Mikael Kågebäck, Olof Mogren, Nina Tahmasebi and Devdatt Dubhashi |
| 15:10–15:30 | *Investigating the Contribution of Distributional Semantic Information for Dialogue Act Classification*<br>Dmitrijs Milajevs and Matthew Purver |
| 15:30–16:00 | Coffee Break |
| 16:00–16:50 | Invited Talk by Phil Blunsom |
| 16:50–17:50 | Panel Discussion with Chris Manning, Phil Blunsom, Ivan Titov and Geoffrey Zweig |

# Post-hoc Manipulations of Vector Space Models with Application to Semantic Role Labeling

**Jenna Kanerva** and **Filip Ginter**
Department of Information Technology
University of Turku, Finland
jmnybl@utu.fi, figint@utu.fi

## Abstract

In this paper, we introduce several vector space manipulation methods that are applied to trained vector space models in a post-hoc fashion, and present an application of these techniques in semantic role labeling for Finnish and English. Specifically, we show that the vectors can be circularly shifted to encode syntactic information and subsequently averaged to produce representations of predicate senses and arguments. Further, we show that it is possible to effectively learn a linear transformation between the vector representations of predicates and their arguments, within the same vector space.

## 1 Introduction

Recently, there has been much progress in the development of highly scalable methods for inducing vector space representations of language. In particular, the *word2vec* method (Mikolov et al., 2013b) is capable of training on billions of tokens in a matter of hours, producing high quality representations. An exciting property exhibited by the vector spaces induced using *word2vec* is that they preserve a number of linguistic regularities, lending themselves to simple algebraic operations with the vectors (Mikolov et al., 2013c) and linear mapping between different spaces (Mikolov et al., 2013a). These can be seen as *post-hoc* operations manipulating the vector space with the significant advantage of not requiring a new task-specific representation to be induced, as is customary.

In this paper, we will investigate several additional such methods. Firstly, we will show how syntax information can be encoded by the circular shift operation and demonstrate that such shifted vectors can be averaged in a meaningful manner to represent predicate arguments. And secondly, we will show that linear transformations of the vector spaces can be successfully applied also within a single vector space, to tasks such as transforming the vector of a predicate into the vector of its argument with a particular role.

To test the above-mentioned operations in an extrinsic setting, we will develop these methods within the context of the Semantic Role Labeling (SRL) task. Automatic Semantic Role Labeling is the process of identifying the semantic arguments of predicates, and assigning them labels describing their roles. A predicate and its arguments form a predicate-argument structure, which describes events such as *who* does *what* to *whom*, *when* and *where*.

The SRL task is "semantic" in its nature and therefore suitable for the application and testing of vector space representations and methods for their manipulation. However, rather than merely adding features derived from vector spaces into an existing system, we will approach the development from a different angle and test whether these representations of words and the similarities they induce can be used for predicate argument role assignment and predicate sense disambiguation as the primary source of information, with little additional features.

In addition to the standard English CoNLL'09 dataset, we will apply the methods also to Finnish SRL, testing the applicability of *word2vec* and the overall methodology that we will develop in this paper to this highly inflective language. With its considerably larger and sparser surface form lexicon, Finnish poses interesting challenges of its own, and only little attention has been dedicated to the application of distributional semantics methods specifically to Finnish. This is also partly due to the lack of sufficiently sized corpora, which we address in this work by using a 1.5B token corpus of Internet Finnish.

In order to be able to test the proposed methods on SRL, we need to carry out not only role labeling and predicate sense disambiguation, but also argument detection. As a secondary theme, we thus test whether dependency parse graphs in the semantically motivated Stanford Dependencies (SD) scheme can be used as-is to perform argument identification. We are especially interested in this scheme as it is designed to capture *semantically contentful* relations (de Marneffe and Manning, 2008) and would thus appear to be the ideal choice as the underlying syntactic representation for SRL.

## 2 Data and Task Setting

Throughout the paper, we will use the exact same task setting as in the CoNLL'09 Shared Task on Syntactic and Semantic Dependencies in Multiple Languages (Hajič et al., 2009). The input of the SRL system are automatically generated syntactic parses and the list of predicate tokens to be considered in each sentence. For each of the predicates, the SRL system is expected to predict the *sense* of the predicate, identify all tokens which are its arguments, and for each argument, identify its role. As the primary measure of performance, we will use the *semantic F-score* defined in the CoNLL shared task. This F-score is calculated from the precision and recall of argument identification (calculated in the obvious manner) and also incorporates the sense of the predicate via an additional "dummy" argument. We use the official implementation of the metric distributed on the Shared Task site.[1]

We will report our results on two SRL datasets: the *Finnish PropBank* (Haverinen et al., 2013a) and the English SRL dataset from the CoNLL'09 Shared Task. The Finnish PropBank is built on top of the *Turku Dependency Treebank (TDT)*, a 205K token corpus of general Finnish (Haverinen et al., 2013b) annotated using the SD scheme, including manually annotated conjunct propagation and other dependency relations from the non-basic layer of the scheme. These extended SD analyzes are thus not strictly trees, rather they are directed labeled graphs (see Figure 1). The Finnish PropBank has 22 different argument roles of which 7 are numbered core roles and 15 are modifier roles. The Finnish data has 164,530 training tokens with 27,603 occurrences of 2,826 unique predicate-

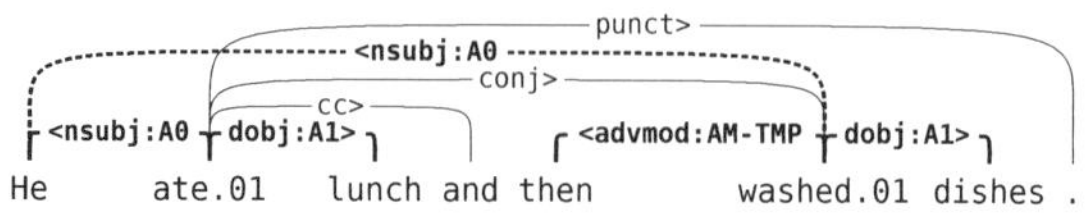


Figure 1: Extended Stanford Dependencies scheme combined with PropBank annotation.

sense combinations. The English CoNLL data is derived from the PropBank and NomBank corpora (Palmer et al., 2005; Meyers et al., 2004) and it has a total of 54 different argument roles. In addition to the same 22 roles as Finnish, English also has discontinuous variants for each role. The English data has 958,024 training tokens with 178,988 occurrences of 15,880 unique predicate-sense combinations.

All Finnish results are reported on the test subset of the Finnish PropBank, and have no previously published baseline to compare with. The results we report for English are produced on the official test section of the CoNLL'09 data and are thus directly comparable to the official results reported in the Shared Task.

In the test phase, we follow the Shared Task setting whereby morphological and syntactic analysis is predicted as well, i.e., no gold standard data enters the system other than the tokenization and the information of which tokens constitute predicates. We produce the Finnish morphological and syntactic analyses for the test set with the parsing pipeline of Haverinen et al. (2013b), composed of a morphological analyzer and tagger (Halácsy et al., 2007; Pirinen, 2008; Lindén et al., 2009), dependency parser (Bohnet, 2010) and a machine-learning based component for predicting the extended SD dependencies (Nyblom et al., 2013). While the English data is provided with automatically produced dependency parses, we are specifically interested in the SD scheme and therefore we re-parse the corpus with the Stanford parser[2] taking a union of the base and collapsed dependency outputs to match the Finnish data.

The vector space models used throughout this paper are induced using the *word2vec* software (skip-gram architecture with default parameters). For Finnish, the model is trained on 1.5 billion tokens of Finnish Internet texts gathered from the *Common Crawl* dataset.[3] The data was sentence-

[1] http://ufal.mff.cuni.cz/conll2009-st/scorer.html

[2] Version 3.3.1, October 2013

[3] http://commoncrawl.org/

split and tokenized using the OpenNLP[4] toolchain trained on TDT, and processed in the same manner as the above-mentioned test set. This gives us the opportunity to build two models, one for the word forms and the other for the lemmas. Both Finnish models have 300 dimensions. For English, the vector representation is induced on the union of the English Wikipedia (1.7B tokens) and the English Gigaword corpus (4B tokens), the total training data size thus being 5.7 billion tokens.[5] Sentence splitting and tokenization was carried out using the relevant modules from the *BRAT* package (Stenetorp et al., 2012).[6] The English model has 200 dimensions.

## 3 Method

In this section, we will describe the methods developed for argument identification, argument role labeling and predicate sense disambiguation, the three steps that must be implemented to obtain a full SRL system.

### 3.1 Argument identification

In a semantically-oriented dependency scheme, such as SD, it can be expected that a notable proportion of arguments (in the SRL sense) are directly attached to the predicate, and argument identification can be reduced to assuming that — with a limited number of systematic exceptions — every argument is a dependent of the predicate. The most frequent case where the assumption does not hold in Finnish are the copula verbs, which are not analyzed as heads in the SD scheme. For English, a common case are the auxiliaries, which govern the main verb in the CoNLL data and are thus marked as arguments for other higher-level predicates as well. In the SD scheme, on the other hand, the main verb governs the auxiliary taking also its place in the syntactic tree. Since the focus of this paper lies in role assignment, we do not go beyond developing a simple rule set to deal with a limited number of such cases. In Section 6, we will contrast this simple argument identification method to that of the winning CoNLL'09 system and we will show that while for Finnish the above holds surprisingly well, the performance on the English data is clearly sub-optimal.

[4]`http://opennlp.apache.org/`

[5]We are thankful to Sampo Pyysalo for providing us with the English *word2vec* model.

[6]`http://brat.nlplab.org`

| **Finnish** | |
|---|---|
| eat + A1 | AM-TMP |
| salted fish | not until |
| eggs | now |
| wheat bread | again |
| nuts | when |
| pickled cucumbers | then |
| **English** | |
| drive + A1 | drive + AM-TMP |
| car | immediately |
| truck | morning |
| cars | now |
| vehicle | afternoon |
| tires | finally |

Table 1: Five most similar words for the given average argument vectors. *AM-TMP* refers to the temporal modifier role. Note that the average vectors for Finnish modifier roles are estimated independently from the predicates (see Section 3.4).

### 3.2 Role Classification

Our initial role classification algorithm is based on calculating the vector representation of an "average argument" with a given role. For every predicate $x$ and every role $r$, we calculate the representation of the average argument with the role as

$$A(x, r) = \frac{\sum_{(r,x,y)} \hat{y}}{count}, \quad (1)$$

where $\hat{y}$ refers to the L2 normalized version of $y$, and *count* to the number of training pairs that are summed over. We are thus averaging the normalized vectors of all words $y$ seen in the training data as an argument of the predicate $x$ with the role $r$. To establish the role for some argument $y$ during testing, we can simply choose the role whose average argument vector has the maximal similarity to $y$, i.e.

$$\arg\max_r sim(A(x, r), y), \quad (2)$$

where $sim(a, b)$ is the standard cosine similarity.

To gain an intuitive insight into whether the average argument vectors behave as expected, we show in Table 1 the top five most similar words to the average argument vectors for several roles and predicates. When evaluated with the data sets described in Section 2, this initial method leads to 61.32% semantic F-score for Finnish and 65.05% for English.

### 3.3 Incorporating syntax

As we will demonstrate shortly, incorporating information about dependency relations can lead to a substantial performance gain. To incorporate the dependency relation information into the role classification method introduced above, we apply the technique of circular shifting of vectors. This technique was previously used in the context of *Random Indexing (RI)* to derive new vectors from existing ones in a deterministic fashion (Basile and Caputo, 2012). In RI, the shift operation is however not used on the final vectors, but rather already during the induction of the vector representation.

Given a vector representation of an argument $y$, we can encode the dependency relation of $y$ and its predicate by circularly shifting the vector of $y$ by an offset assigned separately to each possible dependency relation. The assignment is arbitrary, but such that no two relations are assigned the same offset. We will denote this operation as $y \gg d$, meaning the vector $y$ circularly shifted to the right by the offset assigned to the dependency relation $d$. For instance, circularly shifting a vector $a = (1, 2, 3, 4, 5)$ to the right by an offset of 2 results in $a \gg 2 = (4, 5, 1, 2, 3)$.

We can incorporate the dependency relations when calculating the average vectors representing arguments as follows:

$$A(x, r) = \frac{\sum_{(r,d,x,y)} \hat{y} \gg d}{count}, \qquad (3)$$

where $(r, d, x, y)$ iterates over all predicate-argument pairs $(x, y)$ where $y$ has the dependency relation $d$ and role $r$. The role of an argument in the test phase is established as before, by taking the role which maximizes the similarity to the average vector:

$$\arg\max_r sim(A(x, r), y \gg d) \qquad (4)$$

In the cases, where arguments are not direct dependents of the predicate, we use zero as the shift offset.

To motivate this approach and illustrate its implications, consider the two sentences (1) *The cat chases the dog.* (2) *The dog chases the cat.* In the first sentence the *dog* is an object which corresponds to the theme role *A1*, whereas in the second sentence it is a subject with the agent role *A0*. The role labeling decision is, however, in both cases based on the similarity value $sim(A(chases, r), dog)$, predicting *A1*, which is incorrect in the latter case. When we incorporate the syntactic information by shifting the vector according to its syntactic relation to the predicate, we obtain two diverging similarity values because $dog \gg nsubj$ and $dog \gg dobj$ are essentially two different vectors. This leads to the correct prediction in both cases.

Relative to the base method, incorporating the syntax improves the semantic F-score from 61.32% to 66.23% for Finnish and from 65.05% to 66.55% for English. For Finnish, the gain is rather substantial, while for English we see only a moderate but nevertheless positive effect. This demonstrates that, indeed, the circular shifting operation successfully encodes syntactic information both into the average vectors $A$ and the candidate argument vectors $y$.

### 3.4 Core arguments vs. modifiers

In comparison to modifier roles, the assignment of core (numbered) argument roles is considerably more influenced by the predicate sense and therefore must be learned separately, which we also confirmed in initial experiments. The modifier roles, on the other hand, are global in the sense that they are not tied to any particular predicate. This brings out an interesting question of whether the modifier roles should be learned independently of the predicate or not. We find that the best strategy is to learn predicate-specific modifier vectors in English and global modifier vectors in Finnish.

Another problem, particularly common in the Finnish PropBank stems from the distinction between core roles and modifier roles. For instance, for the predicate *to move* the argument meaning the destination of the moving action has the core role *A2*, while for a number of other predicates which may optionally take a destination argument, the directional modifier role *AM-DIR* would be used. This leads to a situation where core arguments receive a high score for a modifier role, and modifier roles are over-predicted at the expense of core argument roles. To account for this, we introduce the following simple heuristics. If the predicate lacks a core role $r$ after prediction, iterate through predicted modifier roles $p_1 \ldots p_n$ and change the prediction from $p_i$ to $r$ if $r$ has the maximum similarity among the core roles and the difference $sim(p_i, y) - sim(r, y)$ is smaller than a threshold value optimized on a held-out development set distinct from the test set.

We observe a 2.05pp gain in Finnish when using this method, whereas in English this feature is less significant with an improvement of only 0.3pp.

### 3.5 Fall-back for unknown words

The above-mentioned techniques based purely on vector representations with no additional features fail if the vector space model lacks the argument token which prevents the calculation of the necessary similarities. To address this problem, we build separately for each POS a "generic" representation by averaging the vectors of all training data tokens that have the POS and occurred only once. These vectors, representing a typical rare word of a given POS, are then used in place of words missing from the vector space model.

Another solution taking advantage from the vector space representation is used in cases where a predicate is not seen in the training data and therefore we have no information about its argument structure. We query for predicates closest to the unseen predicate and take the average argument vectors from the most similar predicate that was seen during the training.

Together, these two techniques result in a modest gain of approximately 1pp for both languages.

### 3.6 Sense classification

One final step required in SRL is the disambiguation of the sense of the predicate. Here we apply an approach very similar to that used for role classification, whereby for every sense of every predicate, we calculate an average vector representing that sense. This is done as follows: For every predicate sense, we average the vector representations of all dependents and governors[7] of all occurrences of that sense in the training data, circularly shifted to encode their syntactic relation to the predicate. To assign a sense to a predicate during testing, we average the shifted vectors corresponding to its dependents and governors in the sentence, and choose the sense whose average vector is the nearest. Using this approach, we obtain a 84.18% accuracy for Finnish and 92.68% for English, compared to 79.89% and 92.88% without the syntax information. This corresponds to a substantial gain for Finnish but, surprisingly, a small drop for English. For the rare predicates that are not seen in the training data, we have no information about their sense inventory and therefore we simply predict the sense ".01" which is the correct choice in 79.56% of the cases in Finnish and 86.64% in English.

[7]Recall we use the extended SD scheme where a word can have several governors in various situations.

## 4 Role Labeling with Linear Transformations

As we discussed earlier, it was recently shown that the *word2vec* spaces preserve a number of linguistic regularities, and an accurate mapping between two *word2vec*-induced vector spaces can be achieved using a simple linear transformation. Mikolov et al. (2013a) have demonstrated that a linear transformation trained on source-target language word pairs obtained from Google Translate can surprisingly accurately map word vectors from one language to another, with obvious applications to machine translation. It is also worth noting that this is not universally true of all vector space representation methods, as Mikolov et al. have shown for example for Latent Semantic Analysis, which exhibits this property to a considerably lesser extent. In addition to testing the applicability of the *word2vec* method in general, we are specifically interested whether these additional properties can be exploited in the context of SRL. In particular, we will test whether a similar linear vector space transformation can be used to map the vectors of the predicates onto those of their arguments.

More formally, for each role $r$, we will learn a transformation matrix $W_r$ such that for a vector representation $x$ of some predicate, $W_r x$ will be close to the vector representation of its arguments with the role $r$. For instance, if $x$ is the representation of the predicate *(to) eat*, we aim for $W_{A1}x$ to be a vector similar to the vectors representing edible items (role *A1*). The transformation can be trained using the tuples $(r, x, y)$ of predicate $x$ and its argument $y$ with the role $r$ gathered from the training data, minimizing the error

$$\sum_{(x,y)} ||W_r x - y||^2 \quad (5)$$

over all training pairs (separately for each $r$). We minimize the error using the standard stochastic gradient descent method, whereby the transformation matrix is updated separately for each pair $(x, y)$ using the equation

$$W_r \leftarrow W_r - \epsilon(W_r x - y)x^T \quad (6)$$

where $\epsilon$ is the learning rate whose suitable value is selected on the development set. The whole procedure is repeated until convergence is reached, randomly shuffling the training data after each round of training.

Using the transformation, we can establish the most likely role for the argument $y$ of a predicate $x$ as

$$\arg\max_r sim(W_r x, y) \quad (7)$$

where $sim$ is the cosine similarity function, i.e. in the exact same manner as for the average argument method described in the previous section, with the difference that the vector for the average argument is not calculated directly from the training data, but rather obtained through the linear transformation of the predicate vector.

As an alternative approach, we can also learn the reverse transformation $RW_r$ such that $RW_r y$ is close to $x$, i.e. the transformation of the argument $y$ onto the predicate $x$. Note that here $RW_r$ is not the same as $W_r^T$; we train this reverse transformation separately using the same gradient descent method. We then modify the method for finding the most likely role for an argument by taking the average of the forward and reverse transformation similarities:

$$\arg\max_r \frac{sim(W_r x, y) + sim(x, RW_r y)}{2} \quad (8)$$

Note that we make no assumptions about the vector spaces where $x$ and $y$ are drawn from; they may be different spaces and they do not need to be matched in their dimensionality either, as there is no requirement that $W$ and $RW$ be square matrices. In practice, we find that the best strategy for both Finnish and English is to represent both the predicates and arguments using the space induced from word forms, however, we have also tested on Finnish representing the predicates using the space induced from lemmas and the arguments using a space induced from word forms, with only minimally worse results. This shows that the transformation does not degrade substantially even when mapping between two different spaces.

With this strategy, we reach an F-score of 62.71% in Finnish and 63.01% in English. These results are on par with the scores obtained with the average argument method, showing that a linear transformation is effective also in this kind of problems.

To incorporate syntax information, we train transformation matrices $W_{r,d}$ and $RW_{r,d}$ for each dependency relation $d$ rather than relying on the circular shift operation which cannot be captured by linear transformations.[8] As some combinations of $r$ and $d$ may occur only in the test data, we use the matrices $W_r$ and $RW_r$ as a fall-back strategy. In testing, we found that even if the $(r, d)$ combination is known from the training data, a small improvement can be obtained by taking the average of the similarities with and without syntactic information as the final similarity. Incorporating these techniques into the basic linear transformation improves the semantic F-score from 62.71% to 65.88% for Finnish and from 63.01% to 67.04% for English. The improvement for both languages is substantial.

## 5 Supervised classification approach

In the previous sections, we have studied an approach to SRL based purely on the vector space representations with no additional features. We have addressed the choice of the argument role by simply assigning the role with the maximum similarity to the argument. To test the gain that could be obtained by employing a more advanced technique for aggregating the scores and incorporating additional features, we train a linear multi-class support vector machine to assign the role to every detected argument. As features, we use the similarity values for each possible role using the best performing method for each language,[9] the sense of the predicate, and — separately for the predicate and the argument — the token itself, its POS, morphological tags, every dependency relation to its governors, and every dependency relation to its dependents. The similarities are encoded as feature weights, while all other features are binary. We use the multi-class SVM implementation from the SVM-multiclass package (Joachims, 1999), setting the regularization parameter on the development set using a grid search.

For both languages, we observe a notable gain in performance, leading to the best scores so far. In Finnish the improvement in F-score is from 66.23% to 73.83% and in English from 67.04% to 70.38%. However, as we will further discuss in Section 6, in Finnish the contribution of the similarity features is modest.

[8] Note that this does not affect the overall computational cost, as the total number of training examples remains unchanged and the transformation matrices are small in size.

[9] Average vectors for Finnish and transformation for English (Table 2).

| | Finnish | English |
|---|---|---|
| **Average vectors** | | |
| full method | 66.23 | 66.55 |
| –modifier vs. core role | 64.18 | 66.25 |
| –syntax | 61.32 | 65.05 |
| **Linear transformation** | | |
| full method | 65.88 | 67.04 |
| –syntax | 62.71 | 63.01 |
| **Supervised classification** | | |
| full method | 73.83 | 70.38 |
| only similarity features | 64.21 | 65.89 |
| –similarity features | 73.54 | 67.51 |
| –lexical features | 65.51 | 58.42 |

Table 2: Overview of main results and a feature ablation study. *Modifier vs. core role* refers to the algorithm presented in Section 3.4. In the supervised classification part, *-lexical features* refers to the removal of features based on word forms, predicate sense and role similarities.

| Finnish | | English | |
|---|---|---|---|
| n | Recall | n | Recall |
| 1 | 58.23 | 1 | 67.39 |
| 2 | 68.29 | 2 | 82.82 |
| 3 | 74.30 | 3 | 88.49 |
| 4 | 78.71 | 4 | 91.58 |
| 5 | 82.21 | 5 | 93.20 |
| 6 | 84.74 | 6 | 94.29 |
| 7 | 87.04 | 7 | 94.91 |
| 8 | 88.98 | 8 | 95.31 |
| 9 | 90.76 | 9 | 95.65 |
| 10 | 92.05 | 10 | 95.86 |

Table 3: A study of how many times (%) the correct role is among the top *n* most similar roles when the arguments are known in advance. Left: Similarities taken from the average vector method on Finnish. Right: Similarities from the linear transformation method on English.

| | Finnish | English |
|---|---|---|
| Average vectors | 66.23 / 89.89 | 66.55 / 79.57 |
| Linear transf. | 65.88 / 89.92 | 67.04 / 80.85 |
| Supervised | 73.83 / 89.29 | 70.38 / 78.71 |

Table 4: Overall results separately for all main methods (labeled/unlabeled semantic F-score).

## 6 Results and discussion

All results discussed throughout Sections 3 to 5 are summarized in Table 2, which also serves as a coarse feature ablation study. Overall, we see that the average vector and linear transformation methods perform roughly on par, with the average vector method being slightly better for Finnish and slightly worse for English. Both vector space-based methods gain notably from syntax information, confirming that the manner in which this information is incorporated is indeed meaningful.

Adding the SVM classifier on top of these two methods results in a substantial further raise in performance, demonstrating that to be competitive on SRL, it is necessary to explicitly model also additional information besides the semantic similarity between the predicate and the argument. This is particularly pronounced for Finnish where the present SVM method does not gain substantially from the similarity-based features, while English clearly benefits. To shed some light on this difference, we show in Table 3 the oracle accuracy of role labeling for top-1 through top-10 roles as ordered by their similarity scores. The performance on English is clearly superior to that on Finnish. An important factor may be the fact that — in terms of token count — the CoNLL'09 English training size is nearly six times that of the Finnish PropBank and the English vector space model was induced on a nearly four times larger text corpus.

Returning to our original question of whether the SD scheme can be used as-is for argument identification, we show in Table 4 the unlabeled F-scores for the main methods. These scores reflect the performance of the argument identification step in isolation. While Finnish approaches 90% which is comparable to the best systems in the CoNLL'09 task, English lags behind by over 10pp. To test to what extent the results would be affected if a more accurate argument identification system was applied, we used the output of the winning (for English) CoNLL'09 Shared Task system (Zhao et al., 2009a) as the argument identification component, while predicting the roles with the methods introduced so far. The results are summarized in Table 5, where we see a substantial gain for all the methods presented in this paper, achieving an F-score of 82.33%, only 3.82pp lower than best CoNLL'09 system. These results give a mixed signal as to whether the extended SD scheme is usable nearly as-is for argument identification (Finnish) or not (English). Despite our efforts, we were unable to pinpoint the cause for this difference, beyond the fact that the Finnish Prop-

| | Semantic F-score |
|---|---|
| CoNLL'09 best | 86.15 / 91.97 |
| Average vectors | 73.12 / 91.97 |
| Linear transformation | 74.41 / 91.97 |
| Supervised classif. | 82.33 / 91.97 |

Table 5: Performance of suggested methods with argument identification from the top-performing CoNLL'09 system (labeled/unlabeled F-score).

Bank was originally developed specifically on top of the SD scheme, while the English PropBank and NomBank corpora were not.

## 7 Related work

While different methods have been studied to build task specific vector space representations, post-hoc methods to manipulate the vector spaces without retraining are rare. Current SRL systems utilize supervised machine learning approaches, and typically a large set of features. For instance, the winning system in the CoNLL'09 shared task (SRL-only) introduces a heavy feature engineering system, which has about 1000 potential feature templates from which the system discovers the best set to be used (Zhao et al., 2009b). Word similarities are usually introduced to SRL as a part of unsupervised or semi-supervised methods. For example, Titov and Klementiev (2012) present an unsupervised clustering method applying word representation techniques, and Deschacht and Moens (2009) used vector similarities to automatically expand the small training set to build semi-supervised SRL system. Additionally, Turian et al. (2010) have shown that word representations can be included among the features to improve the performance of named entity recognition and chunking systems.

## 8 Conclusions

We set out to test two post-hoc vector space manipulation techniques in the context of semantic role labeling. We found that the circular shift operation can indeed be applied also to other vector representations as a way to encode syntactic information. Importantly, the circular shift is applied to a pre-existing vector space representation, rather than during its induction, and is therefore task-independent. Further, we find that such shifted vectors can be meaningfully averaged to represent predicate senses and arguments.

We also extended the study of the linear transformation between two vector spaces and show that the same technique can be used also within a single space, mapping the vectors of predicates onto the vectors of their arguments. This mapping produces results that are performance-wise on par with the average vectors method, demonstrating a good generalization ability of the linear mapping and the underlying *word2vec* vector space representation. Here it is worth noting that — if we gloss over some obvious issues of ambiguity — the mapping between two languages demonstrated by Mikolov et al. is conceptually a one-to-one mapping, at least in contrast to the one-to-many nature of the mapping between predicates and their arguments. These results hint at the possibility that a number of problems which can be reduced to the "predict a word given a word" pattern may be addressable with this simple technique.

With respect to the application to SRL, we have shown that it is possible to carry out SRL based purely on the vector space manipulation methods introduced in this paper, outperforming several entries in the CoNLL-09 Shared Task. However, it is perhaps not too surprising that much more is needed to build a competitive SRL system. Adding an SVM classifier with few relatively simple features derived from the syntactic analyses in addition to features based on vector similarities, and especially adding a well-performing argument identification method, can result in a system close to approaching state-of-the-art performance, which is encouraging.

As future work, it will be interesting to study to which extent SRL, and similar applications would benefit from addressing the one-to-many nature of the underlying problem. While for some predicates the arguments likely form a cluster that can be represented as a single average vector, for other predicates, such as *to see*, it is not the case. Finding methods which allow us to model this property of the problem will constitute an interesting direction with broader applications beyond SRL.

## Acknowledgements

This work has been supported by the Emil Aaltonen Foundation and Kone Foundation. Computational resources were provided by CSC – IT Center for Science. We would also like to thank Sampo Pyysalo and Hans Moen for comments and general discussion.

## References


Pierpaolo Basile and Annalina Caputo. 2012. Encoding syntactic dependencies using Random Indexing and Wikipedia as a corpus. In *Proceedings of the 3rd Italian Information Retrieval (IIR) Workshop*, volume 835, pages 144–154.

Bernd Bohnet. 2010. Very high accuracy and fast dependency parsing is not a contradiction. In *Proceedings of the 23rd International Conference on Computational Linguistics*, pages 89–97. Association for Computational Linguistics.

Koen Deschacht and Marie-Francine Moens. 2009. Semi-supervised semantic role labeling using the latent words language model. In *Proceedings of the 2009 Conference on Empirical Methods in Natural Language Processing: Volume 1-Volume 1*, pages 21–29. Association for Computational Linguistics.

Jan Hajič, Massimiliano Ciaramita, Richard Johansson, Daisuke Kawahara, Maria Antònia Martí, Lluís Màrquez, Adam Meyers, Joakim Nivre, Sebastian Padó, Jan Štěpánek, et al. 2009. The CoNLL-2009 shared task: Syntactic and semantic dependencies in multiple languages. In *Proceedings of the Thirteenth Conference on Computational Natural Language Learning: Shared Task*, pages 1–18. Association for Computational Linguistics.

Péter Halácsy, András Kornai, and Csaba Oravecz. 2007. HunPos: an open source trigram tagger. In *Proceedings of the 45th annual meeting of the ACL on interactive poster and demonstration sessions*, pages 209–212. Association for Computational Linguistics.

Katri Haverinen, Veronika Laippala, Samuel Kohonen, Anna Missilä, Jenna Nyblom, Stina Ojala, Timo Viljanen, Tapio Salakoski, and Filip Ginter. 2013a. Towards a dependency-based PropBank of general Finnish. In *Proceedings of the 19th Nordic Conference on Computational Linguistics (NoDaLiDa'13)*, pages 41–57.

Katri Haverinen, Jenna Nyblom, Timo Viljanen, Veronika Laippala, Samuel Kohonen, Anna Missilä, Stina Ojala, Tapio Salakoski, and Filip Ginter. 2013b. Building the essential resources for Finnish: the Turku Dependency Treebank. *Language Resources and Evaluation*, pages 1–39.

Thorsten Joachims. 1999. Making large-scale SVM learning practical. In *Advances in Kernel Methods - Support Vector Learning*, pages 169–184. MIT Press.

Krister Lindén, Miikka Silfverberg, and Tommi Pirinen. 2009. HFST tools for morphology — an efficient open-source package for construction of morphological analyzers. In *State of the Art in Computational Morphology*, volume 41 of *Communications in Computer and Information Science*, pages 28–47.

Marie-Catherine de Marneffe and Christopher D. Manning. 2008. The Stanford typed dependencies representation. In *Coling 2008: Proceedings of the workshop on Cross-Framework and Cross-Domain Parser Evaluation*, pages 1–8. Coling 2008 Organizing Committee.

Adam Meyers, Ruth Reeves, Catherine Macleod, Rachel Szekely, Veronika Zielinska, Brian Young, and Ralph Grishman. 2004. The NomBank project: An interim report. In *HLT-NAACL 2004 Workshop: Frontiers in Corpus Annotation*, pages 24–31.

Tomas Mikolov, Quoc V. Le, and Ilya Sutskever. 2013a. Exploiting similarities among languages for machine translation. *CoRR (arxiv.org)*, abs/1309.4168.

Tomas Mikolov, Ilya Sutskever, Kai Chen, Greg S. Corrado, and Jeff Dean. 2013b. Distributed representations of words and phrases and their compositionality. In *Advances in Neural Information Processing Systems 26*, pages 3111–3119.

Tomas Mikolov, Wen-tau Yih, and Geoffrey Zweig. 2013c. Linguistic regularities in continuous space word representations. In *Proceedings of the 2013 Conference of the North American Chapter of the Association for Computational Linguistics: Human Language Technologies*, pages 746–751. Association for Computational Linguistics, June.

Jenna Nyblom, Samuel Kohonen, Katri Haverinen, Tapio Salakoski, and Filip Ginter. 2013. Predicting conjunct propagation and other extended Stanford Dependencies. In *Proceedings of the International Conference on Dependency Linguistics (Depling 2013)*, pages 252–261.

Martha Palmer, Daniel Gildea, and Paul Kingsbury. 2005. The proposition bank: An annotated corpus of semantic roles. *Computational Linguistics*, 31(1):71–106.

Tommi Pirinen. 2008. Suomen kielen äärellistilainen automaattinen morfologinen jäsennin avoimen lähdekoodin resurssein. Master's thesis, University of Helsinki.

Pontus Stenetorp, Sampo Pyysalo, Goran Topić, Tomoko Ohta, Sophia Ananiadou, and Jun'ichi Tsujii. 2012. BRAT: a web-based tool for nlp-assisted text annotation. In *Proceedings of the Demonstrations at the 13th Conference of the European Chapter of the Association for Computational Linguistics*, pages 102–107. Association for Computational Linguistics.

Ivan Titov and Alexandre Klementiev. 2012. A Bayesian approach to unsupervised semantic role induction. In *Proceedings of the 13th Conference of the European Chapter of the Association for Computational Linguistics*, pages 12–22. Association for Computational Linguistics.

Joseph Turian, Lev Ratinov, and Yoshua Bengio. 2010. Word representations: a simple and general method for semi-supervised learning. In *Proceedings of the 48th Annual Meeting of the Association for Computational Linguistics*, pages 384–394. Association for Computational Linguistics.

Hai Zhao, Wenliang Chen, Jun'ichi Kazama, Kiyotaka Uchimoto, and Kentaro Torisawa. 2009a. Multilingual dependency learning: Exploiting rich features for tagging syntactic and semantic dependencies. In *Proceedings of the Thirteenth Conference on Computational Natural Language Learning: Shared Task*, pages 61–66. Association for Computational Linguistics.

Hai Zhao, Wenliang Chen, Chunyu Kit, and Guodong Zhou. 2009b. Multilingual dependency learning: a huge feature engineering method to semantic dependency parsing. In *Proceedings of the Thirteenth Conference on Computational Natural Language Learning: Shared Task*, pages 55–60. Association for Computational Linguistics.

# Distributional Composition using Higher-Order Dependency Vectors

**Julie Weeds, David Weir** and **Jeremy Reffin**
Department of Informatics
University of Sussex
Brighton, BN1 9QH, UK
{J.E.Weeds, D.J.Weir, J.P.Reffin}@sussex.ac.uk

## Abstract

This paper concerns how to apply compositional methods to vectors based on grammatical dependency relation vectors. We demonstrate the potential of a novel approach which uses higher-order grammatical dependency relations as features. We apply the approach to adjective-noun compounds with promising results in the prediction of the vectors for (held-out) observed phrases.

## 1 Introduction

Vector space models of semantics characterise the meaning of a word in terms of distributional features derived from word co-occurrences. The most widely adopted basis for word co-occurrence is proximity, i.e. that two words (or more generally lexemes) are taken to co-occur when they occur together within a certain sized window, or within the same sentence, paragraph, or document. Lin (1998), in contrast, took the syntactic relationship between co-occurring words into account: the distributional features of a word are based on the word's grammatical dependents as found in a dependency parsed corpus. For example, observing that the word *glass* appears as the indirect object of the verb *fill*, provides evidence that the word *glass* has the distributional feature $\overline{\text{iobj}}$:*fill*, where $\overline{\text{iobj}}$ denotes the inverse indirect object grammatical relation. The use of grammatical dependents as word features has been exploited in the discovery of tight semantic relations, such as synonymy and hypernymy, where an evaluation against a gold standard such as WordNet (Fellbaum, 1998) can be made (Lin, 1998; Weeds and Weir, 2003; Curran, 2004).

Pado and Lapata (2007) took this further by considering not just *direct* grammatical dependents, but also including indirect dependents. Thus, observing the sentence *She filled her glass slowly* would provide evidence that the word *glass* has the distributional feature $\overline{\text{iobj}}$:advmod:*slowly* where $\overline{\text{iobj}}$:advmod captures the indirect dependency relationship between *glass* and *slowly* in the sentence.

Note that Pado and Lapata (2007) included a basis mapping function that gave their framework flexibility as to how to map paths such as $\overline{\text{iobj}}$:advmod:*slowly* onto the basis of the vector space. Indeed, the instantiation of their framework that they adopt in their experiments uses a basis mapping function that removes the dependency path to leave just the word, so $\overline{\text{iobj}}$:advmod:*slowly* would be mapped to *slowly*.

In this paper, we are concerned with the problem of distributional semantic composition. We show that the idea that the distributional semantics of a word can be captured with higher-order dependency relationships, provides the basis for a simple approach to compositional distributional semantics. While our approach is quite general, dealing with arbitrarily high-order dependency relationships, and the composition of arbitrary phrases, in this paper we consider only first and second order dependency relations, and adjective-noun composition.

In Section 2, we illustrate our proposal by showing how second order dependency relations can play a role in computing the semantics of adjective-noun composition. In Section 3 we describe a number of experiments that are intended to evaluate the approach, with the results presented in Section 4.

The basis for our evaluation follows Baroni and

Zamparelli (2010) and Guevara (2010). Typically, compositional distributional semantic models can be used to generate an (inferred) distributional vector for a phrase from the (observed) distributional vectors of the phrase's constituents. One of the motivations for doing this is that the observed distributional vectors for most phrases tend to be very sparse, a consequence of the frequency with which typical phrases occur in even large corpora. However, there are phrases that occur sufficiently frequently that a reasonable characterisation of their meaning *can* be captured with their observed distributional vector. Such phrases can be exploited in order to assess the quality of a model of composition. This is achieved by measuring the distributional similarity of the observed and inferred distributional vectors for these high frequency phrases.

The contributions of this paper are as follows. We propose a novel approach to phrasal composition which uses higher order grammatical dependency relations as features. We demonstrate its potential in the context of adjective-noun composition by comparing (held-out) observed and inferred phrasal vectors. Further, we compare different vector operations, different feature association scores and investigate the effect of weighting features before or after composition.

## 2 Composition with Higher-order Dependencies

Consider the problem of adjective-noun composition. For example, what is the meaning of the phrase *small child*? How does it relate to the meanings of the lexemes *small* and *child*? Figure 1 shows a dependency analysis for the sentence *The very small wet child cried loudly.* Tables 1 and 2 show the grammatical dependencies (with other open-class words) for the lexemes *small* and *child* which would be extracted from it.

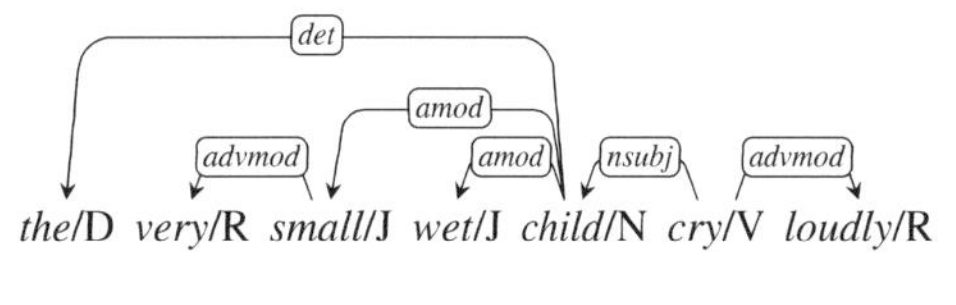


Figure 1: Example Dependency Tree

From Table 1 we see what kinds of (higher-order) dependency paths appear in the distributional features of adjectives such as *small*. Similarly, Table 2 indicates this for nouns such as *child*.

| | |
|---|---|
| 1st-order | advmod:*very*/R<br>$\overline{\text{amod}}$:*child* |
| 2nd-order | $\overline{\text{amod}}$:amod:*wet*/J<br>$\overline{\text{amod}}$:$\overline{\text{nsubj}}$:*cry*/V |
| 3rd-order | $\overline{\text{amod}}$:$\overline{\text{nsubj}}$:advmod:*loudly*/R |

Table 1: Grammatical Dependencies of *small*

| | |
|---|---|
| 1st-order | amod:*wet*/J<br>amod:*small*/J<br>$\overline{\text{nsubj}}$:*cry*/V |
| 2nd-order | amod:advmod:*very*/R<br>$\overline{\text{nsubj}}$:advmod:*loudly*/R |

Table 2: Grammatical Dependencies of *child*

It is clear that with a conventional grammatical dependency-based approach where only first order dependencies for *small* and *child* would be considered, there will be very little overlap between the features of nouns and adjectives because quite different grammatical relations are used in the two types of vectors, and correspondingly lexemes with different parts of speech appear at the end of these paths.

However, as our example illustrates, it is possible to align the 2nd-order feature space of adjectives with the 1st-order feature space of nouns. In this example, we have evidence that *children cry* and that *small* things *cry*. Consequently, in order to compose an adjective with a noun, we would want to align 2nd-order features of the adjective with 1st-order features of the noun; this gives us a prediction of the first order features of the noun in the context of the adjective[1].

This idea extends in a straightforward way beyond adjective-noun composition. For example, it is possible to align the 3rd order features of adjectives with 2nd order features of nouns, which is something that would be useful if one wanted to compose verbs with their arguments. These arguments will include adjective-noun compounds and therefore adjective-noun compounds require 2nd-order features which can be aligned with the first order features of the verbs. This is, however, not

[1]Note that it would also be possible to align 2nd-order features of the noun with 1st-order features of the adjective, resulting in a prediction of the first order features of the adjective in the context of the noun.

something that we will pursue further in this paper.

We now clarify how features vectors are aligned and then composed. Suppose that the lexemes $w_1$ and $w_2$ which we wish to compose are connected by relation $r$. Let $w_1$ be the head of the relation and $w_2$ be the dependent. In our example, $w_1$ is *child*, $w_2$ is *small* and $r$ is amod. We first produce a reduced vector for $w_2$ which is designed to lie in a comparable feature space as the vector for $w_1$. To do this we take the set of 2nd order features of $w_2$ which start with the relation $\bar{r}$ and reduce them to first order features (by removing the $\bar{r}$ at the start of the path). So in our example, we create a reduced vector for *small* where features $\overline{\text{amod}}$:$\overline{\text{nsubj}}$:$x$ for some token $x$ are reduced to $\overline{\text{nsubj}}$:$x$, features $\overline{\text{amod}}$:amod:$x$ for some token $x$ are reduced to the feature amod:$x$, and features $\overline{\text{amod}}$:$\overline{\text{nsubj}}$:advmod:$x$ for some token $x$ are reduced to $\overline{\text{nsubj}}$:advmod:$x$. Once the vector for $w_2$ has been reduced, it can be composed with the vector for $w_1$ using standard vector operations.

In Section 3 we describe experiments that explore the effectiveness of this approach to distributional composition by measuring the similarity of composed vectors with observed vectors for a set of frequently occurring adjective-noun pairs (details given below). We evaluate a number of instantiations of our approach, and in particular, there are three aspects of the model where alternative solutions are available: the choice of which vector composition operation to use; the choice of how to weight dependency features; and the question as to whether feature weighting should take place before or after composition.

**Vector composition operation.** We consider each of the following seven alternatives: pointwise addition (`add`), pointwise multiplication (`mult`), pointwise geometric mean[2] (`gm`), pointwise maximum (`max`), pointwise minimum (`min`), first argument (`hd`), second argument (`dp`). The latter two operations simply return the first (respectively second) of the input vectors.

**Feature weighting.** We consider three options. Much work in this area has used positive pointwise mutual information (PPMI) (Church and Hanks, 1989) to weight the features. However, PPMI is known to over-emphasise low frequency events, and as a result there has been a recent shift towards using positive localised mutual information (PLMI) (Scheible et al., 2013) and positive normalised point wise mutual information (PNPMI) (Bouma, 2009). For definitions, see Table 3.

$$\text{PPMI}(x, y) = \begin{cases} I(x, y) & \text{if } I(x, y) > 0 \\ 0 & \text{otherwise} \end{cases}$$

where $I(x, y) = log\frac{P(x,y)}{P(x).P(y)}$

$$\text{PLMI}(x, y) = \begin{cases} L(x, y) & \text{if } L(x, y) > 0 \\ 0 & \text{otherwise} \end{cases}$$

where $L(x, y) = P(x, y).log(\frac{P(x,y)}{P(x).P(y)}$

$$\text{PNPMI}(x, y) = \begin{cases} N(x, y) & \text{if } N(x, y) > 0 \\ 0 & \text{otherwise} \end{cases}$$

where $N(x, y) = \frac{1}{-log(P(y)}.log\frac{P(x,y)}{P(x).P(y)}$

Table 3: Feature Association Scores

**Timing of feature weighting.** We consider two alternatives: we can weight features before composition so that the composition operation is applied to weighted vectors, or we can compose vectors prior to feature weighting, in which case the composition operation is applied to unweighted vectors, and feature weighting is applied in the context of making a similarity calculation. In other work, the former order is often implied. For example, Boleda et al. (2013) state that they use "PMI to weight the co-occurrence matrix". However, if we allow the second order, features which might have a zero association score in the context of the the individual lexemes, could be considered significant in the context of the phrase.

## 3 Evaluation

Our experimental evaluation of the approach is based on the assumption, which is commonly made elsewhere, that where there is a reasonable amount of corpus data available for a phrase, this will generate a good estimate of the vector of the phrase. It has been shown (Turney, 2012; Baroni and Zamparelli, 2010) that such "observed" vectors are indeed reasonable for adjective-noun and noun-noun compounds. Hence, in order to evaluate the compositional models under consideration here, we compare observed phrasal vectors with inferred phrasal vectors, where the comparison is made using the cosine measure. We note that it is

[2]The geometric mean of $x$ and $y$ is $\sqrt(x \cdot y)$.

not possible to draw conclusions from the absolute value of the cosine score since this would favour models which always assign higher cosine scores. Hence, we draw conclusions from the change in cosine score with respect to a baseline within the same model.

### Methodology

For each noun and adjective which occur more than a threshold number of times in a corpus, we first extract conventional first order dependency vectors. The features of these lexemes define the semantic space, and feature probabilities (for use in association scores) are calculated from this data.

Given a list of adjective-noun phrases, we extract first order vectors for the nouns and second order vectors for the adjectives, which we refer to as observed constituent vectors. We also extract first order vectors for the nouns in the context of the adjective, which we refer to as the observed phrasal vector.

For each adjective-noun pair, we build bespoke constituent vectors for the adjective and noun, in which we remove all counts which arise from co-occurrences with that specific adjective-noun pair. It is these constituent vectors that are used as the basis for inferring the vector for that particular adjective-noun phrase.

Our rationale for this is as follows. Without this modification, the observed constituent vectors will contain co-occurrences which are due to the observed adjective-noun vector co-occurrences. To see why this is undesirable, suppose that one of the adjective-noun phrases was *small child*. We take the observed vector for *small child* to be what we are calling the observed phrasal vector for *child* (in the context of *small*). Suppose that when building the observed phrasal vector, we observe the phrase *the small child cried*. This will lead to a count for the feature $\overline{\mathsf{nsubj}}$:*cry* in the observed phrasal vector for *child*.

But if we are not careful, this same phrase will contribute to counts in the *constituent* vectors for *small* and *child*, producing counts for the features $\overline{\mathsf{amod}}$:$\overline{\mathsf{nsubj}}$:*cry* and $\overline{\mathsf{nsubj}}$:*cry*, in their respective vectors. To see why these counts should not be included when building the constituent vectors that we compose to produce inferred vectors for the adjective-noun phrase *small child*, consider the case where all of the evidence for *small* things being things that can *cry* and *children* being things that can *crying* comes from having observed the phrase *small children crying*. Despite not having learnt anything about the composition of *small* and *child* in general, we would be able to infer the *cry* feature for the phrase. An adequate model of composition should be able to infer this on the basis that other *small* things have been seen to *cry*, and that non-*small children* have been seen to *cry*.

Here, we compare the proposed approach, based on higher order dependencies, with the standard method of composing conventional first-order dependency vectors. The vector operation, `hd` provides a baseline for comparison which is the same in both approaches. This baseline corresponds to a composition model where the first order dependencies of the phrase (i.e. the noun in the context of the adjective) are taken to be the same as the first order dependencies of the uncontextualized noun. For example, if we have never seen the phrase *small child* before, we would assume that it means the same as the head word *child*.

We hypothesise that it is not possible to improve on this baseline using traditional first-order dependency relation vectors, since the vector for the modifier does not contain features of the right type, but that with the proposed approach, the inferred vector for a phrase such as *small child* will be closer than observed vector for *child* to the observed vector for *small child*. We also ask the related question of whether our inferred vector for *small child* is closer than the constituent vector for *small* to the observed vector for *small child*. This comparison is achieved through use of the vector operation `dp` that ignores the vector for the head, simply returning a first-order vector derived from the dependent.

### Experimental Settings

Our corpus is a mid-2011 dump of WikiPedia. This has been part-of-speech tagged, lemmatised and dependency parsed using the Malt Parser (Nivre, 2004). All major grammatical dependency relations involving open class parts of speech (nsubj, dobj, iobj, conj, amod, advmod, nnmod) have been extracted for all POS-tagged and lemmatised nouns and adjectives occurring 100 or more times. In past work with conventional dependency relation vectors we found that using a feature threshold of 100, weighting features with PPMI and a cosine similarity score work well.

For experimental purposes, we have taken

| | | | |
|---|---|---|---|
| spanish | british | african | japanese |
| modern | classical | female | natural |
| digital | military | medical | musical |
| scientific | free | black | white |
| heavy | common | small | large |
| strong | short | long | good |
| similar | previous | future | original |
| former | subsequent | next | possible |

Table 4: Adjectives considered

32 of the most frequently occurring adjectives (see Table 4). These adjectives include ones which would generally be considered intersective (e.g., *female*), subsective (e.g,, *long*) and non-subsective/intensional (e.g., *former*) (Pustejovsky, 2013) . For all of these adjectives there are at least 100 adjective-noun phrases which occur at least 100 times in the corpus. We randomly selected 50 of the phrases for each adjective. Note that our proposed method does not require any hyper parameters to be set during training, nor does it require a certain number of phrases per adjective. For the purpose of these experiments we have a list of 1600 adjective-noun phrases, all of which occur at least 100 times in WikiPedia.

## 4 Results and Discussion

Tables 5 and 6 summarise the average cosines for the proposed higher-order dependency approach and the conventional first-order dependency approach, respectively. In each case, we consider each combination of vector operation, feature association score, and composition timing (i.e. before, or after, vector weighting).

Table 7 shows the average improvement over the baseline (`hd`), for each combination of experimental variables, when considering the proposed higher-order dependency approach. Note that this is an average of paired differences (and not the difference of the averages in Table 6). For brevity, we omit the results for PNPMI here, since there do not appear to be substantial differences between using PPMI and PNPMI. To indicate statistical significance, we show estimated standard errors in the means. All differences are statistically significant (under a paired t-test) except those marked †.

From Table 5, we see that none of the compositional operations on conventional dependency vectors are able to beat the baseline of selecting the head vector (`hd`). This is independent of the choice of association measure and the order in which weighting and composition are carried out.

For the higher order dependency vectors (Tables 6 and 7), we note, in contrast, that some compositional operations produce large increases in cosine score compared to the head vector alone (`hd`). Table 7 examines the statistical significance of these differences. We find that for the intersective composition operations (`mult`, `min`, and `gm`), performance is statistically superior to using the head alone in all experimental conditions studied. By contrast, additive measures (`add`, `max`) typically have no impact, or decrease performance marginally relative to the head alone. An explanation for these significant differences is that intersective vector operations are able to encapsulate the way that an adjective disambiguates and specialises the sense of the noun that it is modifying.

We also note that the alternative baseline, `dp`, which estimates the features of a phrase to be the aggregation of all things which are modified by the adjective, performs significantly worse than the standard baseline, `hd`, which estimates the features of a phrase to be the features of the head noun. This is consistent with the intuition that the distributional vector for *small child* should more similar to the vector for *child* than it is to the vector for the things that can be *small.*

Considering the different intersective operations, `mult` appears to be the best choice when the feature association score is PPMI or PNPMI and `gm` appears to be the best choice when the feature association score is PLMI.

Further, PLMI consistently gives all of the vector pairings higher cosine scores than PPMI. Since PLMI assigns less weight to low frequency event and more weight to high frequency events, this suggests that all of the composition methods, including the baseline (`hd`), do better at predicting the high frequency co-occurrences. This is not surprising as these will more likely have been seen with the phrasal constituents in other contexts.

Our final observation, based on Table 6, is that the best order in which to carry out weighting and composition appears to depend on the choice of feature association score. In general, it appears better to weight the features and then compose vectors. This is always true when using PNPMI or PLMI. However, using PPMI, the highest performance is achieved by composing the raw vectors using multiplication and then weighing the

| | weight:compose | | | | | | compose:weight | | | | | |
|---|---|---|---|---|---|---|---|---|---|---|---|---|
| | PPMI | | PNPMI | | PLMI | | PPMI | | PNPMI | | PLMI | |
| | $\bar{x}$ | $s$ | $\bar{x}$ | $s$ | $\bar{x}$ | $s$ | $\bar{x}$ | $s$ | $\bar{x}$ | $s$ | $\bar{x}$ | $s$ |
| `add` | 0.12 | (0.06) | 0.13 | (0.05) | 0.15 | (0.16) | 0.11 | (0.05) | 0.12 | (0.06) | 0.22 | (0.20) |
| `max` | 0.12 | (0.06) | 0.13 | (0.05) | 0.15 | (0.16) | 0.11 | (0.05) | 0.12 | (0.06) | 0.22 | (0.20) |
| `mult` | 0.06 | (0.05) | 0.06 | (0.06) | 0.06 | (0.11) | 0.07 | (0.05) | 0.07 | (0.12) | 0.07 | (0.05) |
| `min` | 0.05 | (0.05) | 0.06 | (0.05) | 0.04 | (0.09) | 0.05 | (0.04) | 0.05 | (0.04) | 0.04 | (0.08) |
| `gm` | 0.06 | (0.05) | 0.06 | (0.05) | 0.07 | (0.11) | 0.05 | (0.04) | 0.06 | (0.04) | 0.08 | (0.11) |
| `hd` | **0.13** | (0.07) | **0.15** | (0.07) | **0.28** | (0.22) | **0.13** | (0.07) | **0.15** | (0.07) | **0.28** | (0.22) |

Table 5: Means and Standard Deviations for Cosines Between Observed and Predicted Vectors for Conventional First-Order Dependency Based Approach.

| | weight:compose | | | | | | compose:weight | | | | | |
|---|---|---|---|---|---|---|---|---|---|---|---|---|
| | PPMI | | PNPMI | | PLMI | | PPMI | | PNPMI | | PLMI | |
| | $\bar{x}$ | $s$ | $\bar{x}$ | $s$ | $\bar{x}$ | $s$ | $\bar{x}$ | $s$ | $\bar{x}$ | $s$ | $\bar{x}$ | $s$ |
| `add` | 0.14 | (0.06) | 0.16 | (0.06) | 0.29 | (0.21) | 0.10 | (0.04) | 0.12 | (0.05) | 0.29 | (0.22) |
| `max` | 0.10 | (0.04) | 0.11 | (0.04) | 0.27 | (0.21) | 0.10 | (0.04) | 0.11 | (0.04) | 0.26 | (0.21) |
| `mult` | **0.30** | (0.12) | **0.33** | (0.12) | 0.40 | (0.29) | **0.34** | (0.10) | **0.32** | (0.10) | 0.32 | (0.27) |
| `min` | 0.26 | (0.11) | 0.27 | (0.11) | 0.40 | (0.24) | 0.24 | (0.10) | 0.25 | (0.10) | 0.37 | (0.23) |
| `gm` | 0.27 | (0.11) | 0.29 | (0.11) | **0.46** | (0.20) | 0.26 | (0.10) | 0.27 | (0.10) | **0.44** | (0.22) |
| `dp` | 0.10 | (0.05) | 0.10 | (0.05) | 0.20 | (0.20) | 0.10 | (0.05) | 0.10 | (0.05) | 0.20 | (0.20) |
| `hd` | 0.13 | (0.07) | 0.15 | (0.07) | 0.28 | (0.22) | 0.13 | (0.07) | 0.15 | (0.07) | 0.28 | (0.22) |

Table 6: Means and Standard Deviations for Cosines Between Observed and Predicted Vectors for Proposed Higher-Order Dependency Based Approach

remaining features. This can be explained by considering the recall and precision of the composed vector's prediction of the observed vector. If we compose using `gm` before weighting vectors, we increase the recall of the prediction, but decrease precision. Whether we use PPMI, PNPMI or PLMI, recall of features increases from 88.8% to 99.5% and precision drops from 5.5% to 4.8%. If we compose using `mult` before weighting vectors, contrary to expectation, recall decreases and precision increases. Whether we use PPMI, PNPMI or PLMI, recall of features decreases from 88.8% to 59.4% but precision increases from 5.5% to 18.9%. Hence, multiplication of the raw vectors is causing a lot of potential shared features to be "lost" when the weighting is subsequently carried out (since multiplication stretches out the value space). This leads to an increase in cosines when PPMI is used for weighting, and a decrease in cosines when PLMI is used. Hence, it appears that the features being removed by multiplying the raw vectors before weighting must be low frequency co-occurrences, which are not observed with the phrase.

## 5 Related Work

In this work, we bring together ideas from several different strands of distributional semantics: incorporating syntactic information into the distributional representation of a lexeme; representing phrasal meaning by creating distributional representations through composition; and representing word meaning in context by modifying the distributional representation of a word.

The use of syntactic structure in distributional representations is not new. Two of the earliest proponents of distributional semantics, Lin (1998) and Lee (1999) used features based on first order dependency relations between words in their distributional representations. More recently, Pado and Lapata (2007) propose a semantic space based on dependency paths. This model outperformed traditional word-based models which do not take syntax into account in a synonymy relation detection task and a prevalent sense acquisition task.

The problem of representing phrasal meaning has traditionally been tackled by taking vector representations for words (Turney and Pantel, 2010) and combining them using some function to pro-

| | weight:compose | | | | compose:weight | | | |
|---|---|---|---|---|---|---|---|---|
| | PPMI | | PLMI | | PPMI | | PLMI | |
| | $\bar{x}$ | $s_{\bar{x}}$ | $\bar{x}$ | $s_{\bar{x}}$ | $\bar{x}$ | $s_{\bar{x}}$ | $\bar{x}$ | $s_{\bar{x}}$ |
| `add` | 0.01 | (0.001) | †0.004 | (0.003) | -0.03 | (0.001) | †0.006 | (0.004) |
| `max` | -0.03 | (0.001) | -0.01 | (0.003) | -0.04 | (0.001) | -0.02 | (0.003) |
| `mult` | **0.16** | (0.002) | 0.11 | (0.006) | **0.21** | (0.002) | 0.03 | (0.006) |
| `min` | 0.13 | (0.001) | 0.11 | (0.007) | 0.10 | (0.001) | 0.09 | (0.007) |
| `gm` | 0.14 | (0.001) | **0.18** | (0.005) | 0.12 | (0.001) | **0.16** | (0.005) |
| `dp` | -0.03 | (0.002) | -0.09 | (0.007) | -0.04 | (0.002) | -0.09 | (0.007) |

Table 7: Means and Standard Errors for Increases in Cosine with respect to the `hd` Baseline for Proposed Higher-Order Dependency Based Approach. All differences statistically significant (under a paired t-test) except those marked †.

duce a data structure that represents the phrase or sentence. Mitchell and Lapata (2008, 2010) found that simple additive and multiplicative functions applied to proximity-based vector representations were no less effective than more complex functions when performance was assessed against human similarity judgements of simple paired phrases.

The simple functions evaluated by Mitchell and Lapata (2008) are generally acknowledged to have serious theoretical limitations in their treatment of composition. How can a commutative function such as multiplication or addition provide different interpretations for different word orderings such as *window glass* and *glass window*? The majority of attempts to rectify this have offered a more complex, non-commutative function — such as weighted addition — or taken the view that some or all words are no longer simple vectors. For example, in the work of Baroni and Zamparelli (2010) and Guevara (2010), an adjective is viewed as a modifying function and represented by a matrix. Coecke et al. (2011) and Grefenstette et al. (2013) also incorporate the notion of function application from formal semantics. They derived function application from syntactic structure, representing functions as tensors and arguments as vectors. The MV-RNN model of Socher et al. (2012) broadened the Baroni and Zamparelli (2010) approach; all words, regardless of part-of-speech, were modelled with both a vector and a matrix. This approach also shared features with Coecke et al. (2011) in using syntax to guide the order of phrasal composition. These higher order structures are typically learnt or induced using a supervised machine learning technique. For example, Baroni and Zamparelli (2010) learnt their adjectival matrixes by performing regression analysis over pairs of observed nouns and adjective-noun phrases. As a consequence of the computational expense of the machine learning techniques involved, implementations of these approaches typically require a considerable amount of dimensionality reduction.

A long-standing topic in distributional semantics has been the modification of a canonical representation of a lexeme's meaning to reflect the context in which it is found. Typically, a canonical vector for a lexeme is estimated from all corpus occurrences and the vector then modified to reflect the instance context (Lund and Burgess, 1996; Erk and Padó, 2008; Mitchell and Lapata, 2008; Thater et al., 2009; Thater et al., 2010; Thater et al., 2011; Van de Cruys et al., 2011; Erk, 2012). As described in Mitchell and Lapata (2008, 2010), lexeme vectors have typically been modified using simple additive and multiplicative compositional functions. Other approaches, however, share with our proposal the use of syntax to drive modification of the distributional representation (Erk and Padó, 2008; Thater et al., 2009; Thater et al., 2010; Thater et al., 2011). For example, in the SVS representation of Erk and Padó (2008), a word was represented by a set of vectors: one which encodes its lexical meaning in terms of distributionally similar words[3], and one which encodes the selectional preferences of each grammatical relation it supports. A word's meaning vector was updated in the context of another word by combining it with the appropriate selectional preferences vec-

[3]These are referred to as second-order vectors using the terminology of Grefenstette (1994) and Schütze (1998). However, this refers to a second-order affinity between the words and is not related to the use of grammatical dependency relations.

tor of the contextualising word.

Turney (2012) offered a model of phrasal level similarity which combines assessments of word-level semantic relations. This work used two different word-level distributional representations to encapsulate two types of similarity. Distributional similarity calculated from proximity-based features was used to estimate domain similarity and distributional similarity calculated from syntactic pattern based features is used to estimate functional similarity. The similarity of a pair of compound noun phrases was computed as a function of the similarities of the components. Crucially different from other models of phrasal level similarity, it does not attempt to derive modified vectors for phrases or words in context.

## 6 Conclusions and Further Work

Vectors based on grammatical dependency relations are known to be useful in the discovery of tight semantic relations, such as synonymy and hypernymy, between lexemes (Lin, 1998; Weeds and Weir, 2003; Curran, 2004). It would be useful to be able to extend these methods to determine similarity between phrases (of potentially different lengths). However, conventional approaches to composition, which have been applied to proximity-based vectors, cannot sensibly be used on vectors that are based on grammatical dependency relations.

In our approach, we consider the vector for a phrase to be the vector for the head lexeme in the context of the other phrasal constituents. Like Pado and Lapata (2007), we extend the concept of a grammatical dependency relation feature to include dependency relation paths which incorporate higher-order dependencies between words. We have shown how it is possible to align the dependency path features for words of different syntactic types, and thus produce composed vectors which predict the features of one constituent in the context of the other constituent.

In our experiments with AN compounds, we have shown that these predicted vectors are closer than the head constituent's vector to the observed phrasal vector. We have shown this is true even when the observed phrase is in fact unobserved, i.e. when its co-occurrences do not contribute to the constituents' vectors. Consistent with work using proximity-based vectors, we have found that intersective operations perform substantially better than additive operations. This can be understood by viewing the intersective operations as encapsulating the way that adjectives can specialise the meaning of the nouns that they modify.

We have investigated the interaction between the vector operation used for composition, the feature association score and the timing of applying feature weights. We have found that multiplication works best if using PPMI to weight features, but that geometric mean is better if using the increasingly popular PLMI weighting measure. Whilst applying an intersective composition operation before applying feature weighting does allow more features to be retained in the predicted vector (it is possible to achieve 99.5% recall), in general, this does not correspond with an increase in cosine scores. In general, the corresponding drop in precision (i.e., the over-prediction of unobserved features) causes the cosine to decrease. The one exception to this is using multiplication with the PPMI feature weighting score. Here we actually see a drop in recall, and an increase in precision due to the nature of multiplication and PPMI.

One assumption that has been made throughout the work, is that the observed phrasal vector provides a good estimate of the distributional representation of the phrase and, consequently, the best composition method is the one which returns the most similar prediction. However, in general, we notice that while the recall of the compositional methods is good, the precision is very low. Lack of precision may be due to the prevalence of plausible, but unobserved, co-occurrences of the phrase. Consequently, this introduces uncertainty into the conclusions which can be drawn from a study such as this. Further work is required to develop effective intrinsic and extrinsic evaluations of models of composition.

A further interesting area of study is whether distributional models that include higher-order grammatical dependencies can tell us more about the lexical semantics of a word than the conventional first-order models, for example by distinguishing semantic relations such as synonymy, antonymy, hypernymy and co-hyponymy.

## Acknowledgements

This work was funded by UK EPSRC project EP/IO37458/1 "A Unified Model of Compositional and Distributional Compositional Semantics: Theory and Applications".

## References

Marco Baroni and Roberto Zamparelli. 2010. Nouns are vectors, adjectives are matrices: Representing adjective-noun constructions in semantic space. In *Proceedings of the 2010 Conference on Empirical Methods in Natural Language Processing.*

Gemma Boleda, Marco Baroni, The Nghia Pham, and Louise McNally. 2013. Intensionality was only alleged: On adjective-noun composition in distributional semantics. In *Proceedings of the 10th International Conference on Computational Semantics (IWCS 2013) – Long Papers*, pages 35–46, Potsdam, Germany, March. Association for Computational Linguistics.

Gerlof Bouma. 2009. Normalised (point wise) mutual information in collocation extraction, from form to meaning: Processing texts automatically. In *Proceedings of the Biennial International Conference of the German Society for Computational Linguistics and Language Technology.*

Kenneth Ward Church and Patrick Hanks. 1989. Word association norms, mutual information, and lexicography. In *Proceedings of the 27th Annual Meeting on Association for Computational Linguistics*, ACL '89, pages 76–83, Stroudsburg, PA, USA. Association for Computational Linguistics.

Bob Coecke, Mehrnoosh Sadrzadeh, and Stephen Clark. 2011. Mathematical foundations for a compositional distributed model of meaning. *Linguistic Analysis*, 36(1-4):345–384.

James Curran. 2004. *From Distributional to Semantic Similarity*. Ph.D. thesis, University of Edinburgh.

Katrin Erk and Sebastian Padó. 2008. A structured vector space model for word meaning in context. In *Proceedings of the 2008 Conference on Empirical Methods in Natural Language Processing*, pages 897–906, Honolulu, Hawaii, October. Association for Computational Linguistics.

Katrin Erk. 2012. Vector space models of word meaning and phrase meaning: a survey. *Language and Linguistics Compass*, 6(10):635–653.

Christiane Fellbaum. 1998. *WordNet: An Electronic Lexical Database*. Bradford Books.

Edward Grefenstette, Georgiana Dinu, Yao-Zhong Zhang, Mehrnoosh Sadrzadeh, and Marco Baroni. 2013. Multi-step regression learning for compositional distributional semantics. *Proceedings of the 10th International Conference on Computational Semantics (IWCS 2013).*

Gregory Grefenstette. 1994. Corpus-derived first, second and third-order word affinities. In *Proceedings of Euralex 1994.*

Emiliano Guevara. 2010. A Regression Model of Adjective-Noun Compositionality in Distributional Semantics. In *Proceedings of the ACL GEMS Workshop*, pages 33–37.

Lillian Lee. 1999. Measures of distributional similarity. In *Proceedings of the 37th Annual Meeting of the Association for Computational Linguistics*, pages 25–32, College Park, Maryland, USA, June. Association for Computational Linguistics.

Dekang Lin. 1998. Automatic retrieval and clustering of similar words. In *Proceedings of the 17th International Conference on Computational Linguistings (COLING 1998).*

K. Lund and C. Burgess. 1996. Producing high-dimensional semantic spaces from lexical cooccurrence. *Behavior Research Methods, Instrumentation, and Computers*, 28:203–208.

Jeff Mitchell and Mirella Lapata. 2008. Vector-based models of semantic composition. In *Proceedings of ACL-08: HLT*, pages 236–244, Columbus, Ohio, June. Association for Computational Linguistics.

Jeff Mitchell and Mirella Lapata. 2010. Composition in distributional models of semantics. *Cognitive Science*, 34(8):1388–1429.

Joakim Nivre. 2004. Incrementality in deterministic dependency parsing. In *Proceedings of the ACL Workshop on Incremental Parsing*, pages 50–57.

Sebastian Pado and Mirella Lapata. 2007. Dependency-based construction of semantic space models. *Computational Linguistics*, 33(2):161–199.

James Pustejovsky. 2013. Inference patterns with intensional adjectives. In *Proceedings of the IWCS Workshop on Interoperable Semantic Annotation*, Potsdam,Germany, March. Association for Computational Linguistics.

Silke Scheible, Sabine Schulte im Walde, and Sylvia Springorum. 2013. Uncovering distributional differences between synonyms and antonyms in a word space model. In *Proceedings of the International Joint Conference on Natural Language Processing*, pages 489–497, Nagoya, Japan.

Heinrich Schütze. 1998. Automatic word sense discrimination. *Computational Linguistics*, 24(1):97–123.

Richard Socher, Brody Huval, Christopher D Manning, and Andrew Y Ng. 2012. Semantic compositionality through recursive matrix-vector spaces. In *Proceedings of the 2012 Joint Conference on Empirical Methods in Natural Language Processing and Computational Natural Language Learning*, pages 1201–1211. Association for Computational Linguistics.

Stefan Thater, Georgiana Dinu, and Manfred Pinkal. 2009. Ranking paraphrases in context. In *Proceedings of the 2009 Workshop on Applied Textual Inference*, pages 44–47, Suntec, Singapore, August. Association for Computational Linguistics.

Stefan Thater, Hagen Fürstenau, and Manfred Pinkal. 2010. Contextualizing semantic representations using syntactically enriched vector models. In *Proceedings of the 48th Annual Meeting of the Association for Computational Linguistics*, pages 948–957, Uppsala, Sweden, July. Association for Computational Linguistics.

Stefan Thater, Hagen Frstenau, and Manfred Pinkal. 2011. Word meaning in context: A simple and effective vector model. In *Proceedings of 5th International Joint Conference on Natural Language Processing (IJCNLP 2011)*.

P. D. Turney and P. Pantel. 2010. From frequency to meaning: Vector space models of semantics. *Journal of Artificial Intelligence Research*, 37:141–188.

Peter D. Turney. 2012. Domain and function: A dual-space model of semantic relations and compositions. *Journal of Artificial Intelligence Research*, 44.

Tim Van de Cruys, Thierry Poibeau, and Anna Korhonen. 2011. Latent vector weighting for word meaning in context. In *Proceedings of the 2011 Conference on Empirical Methods in Natural Language Processing*, pages 1012–1022, Edinburgh, Scotland, UK., July. Association for Computational Linguistics.

Julie Weeds and David Weir. 2003. A general framework for distributional similarity. In *Proceedings of the 2003 Conference on Empirical Methods in Natural Language Processing*, pages 81–88, Sapporo, Japan.

# A Systematic Study of Semantic Vector Space Model Parameters

**Douwe Kiela**
University of Cambridge
Computer Laboratory
douwe.kiela@cl.cam.ac.uk

**Stephen Clark**
University of Cambridge
Computer Laboratory
sc609@cam.ac.uk

## Abstract

We present a systematic study of parameters used in the construction of semantic vector space models. Evaluation is carried out on a variety of similarity tasks, including a compositionality dataset, using several source corpora. In addition to recommendations for optimal parameters, we present some novel findings, including a similarity metric that outperforms the alternatives on all tasks considered.

## 1 Introduction

Vector space models (VSMs) represent the meanings of lexical items as vectors in a "semantic space". The benefit of VSMs is that they can easily be manipulated using linear algebra, allowing a degree of similarity between vectors to be computed. They rely on the *distributional hypothesis* (Harris, 1954): the idea that "words that occur in similar contexts tend to have similar meanings" (Turney and Pantel, 2010; Erk, 2012). The construction of a suitable VSM for a particular task is highly parameterised, and there appears to be little consensus over which parameter settings to use.

This paper presents a systematic study of the following parameters:

- vector size;
- window size;
- window-based or dependency-based context;
- feature granularity;
- similarity metric;
- weighting scheme;
- stopwords and high frequency cut-off.

A representative set of semantic similarity datasets has been selected from the literature, including a phrasal similarity dataset for evaluating compositionality. The choice of source corpus is likely to influence the quality of the VSM, and so we use a selection of source corpora. Hence there are two additional "superparameters":

- dataset for evaluation;
- source corpus.

Previous studies have been limited to investigating only a small number of parameters, and using a limited set of source corpora and tasks for evaluation (Curran and Moens, 2002a; Curran and Moens, 2002b; Curran, 2004; Grefenstette, 1994; Pado and Lapata, 2007; Sahlgren, 2006; Turney and Pantel, 2010; Schulte im Walde et al., 2013). Rohde et al. (2006) considered several weighting schemes for a large variety of tasks, while Weeds et al. (2004) did the same for similarity metrics. Stone et al. (2008) investigated the effectiveness of sub-spacing corpora, where a larger corpus is queried in order to construct a smaller sub-spaced corpus (Zelikovitz and Kogan, 2006). Blacoe and Lapata (2012) compare several types of vector representations for semantic composition tasks. The most comprehensive existing studies of VSM parameters — encompassing window sizes, feature granularity, stopwords and dimensionality reduction — are by Bullinaria and Levy (2007; 2012) and Lapesa and Evert (2013).

Section 2 introduces the various parameters of vector space model construction. We then attempt, in Section 3, to answer some of the fundamental questions for building VSMs through a number of experiments that consider each of the selected parameters. In Section 4 we examine how these findings relate to the recent development of distributional compositional semantics (Baroni et al., 2013; Clark, 2014), where vectors for words are combined into vectors for phrases.

## 2 Data and Parameters

Two datasets have dominated the literature with respect to VSM parameters: WordSim353 (Finkelstein et al., 2002) and the TOEFL synonym dataset

| Dataset | Pairings | Words |
|---|---|---|
| RG | 65 | 48 |
| MC | 30 | 39 |
| W353 | 353 | 437 |
| MEN | 3000 | 751 |
| TOEFL | 80 | 400 |
| M&L10 | 324 | 314 |

Table 1: Datasets for evaluation

(Landauer and Dumais, 1997). There is a risk that semantic similarity studies have been overfitting to their idiosyncracies, so in this study we evaluate on a variety of datasets: in addition to WordSim353 (W353) and TOEFL, we also use the Rubenstein & Goodenough (RG) (1965) and Miller & Charles (MC) (1991) data, as well as a much larger set of similarity ratings: the MEN dataset (Bruni et al., 2012). All these datasets consist of human similarity ratings for word pairings, except TOEFL, which consists of multiple choice questions where the task is to select the correct synonym for a target word. In Section 4 we examine our parameters in the context of distributional compositional semantics, using the evaluation dataset from Mitchell and Lapata (2010). Table 1 gives statistics for the number of words and word pairings in each of the datasets.

As well as using a variety of datasets, we also consider three different corpora from which to build the vectors, varying in size and domain. These include the **BNC** (Burnard, 2007) ($10^6$ word types, $10^8$ tokens) and the larger **ukWaC** (Baroni et al., 2009) ($10^7$ types, $10^9$ tokens). We also include a **sub-spaced Wikipedia** corpus (Stone et al., 2008): for all words in the evaluation datasets, we build a subcorpus by querying the top 10-ranked Wikipedia documents using the words as search terms, resulting in a corpus with $10^6$ word types and $10^7$ tokens. For examining the dependency-based contexts, we include the **Google Syntactic N-gram** corpus (Goldberg and Orwant, 2013), with $10^7$ types and $10^{11}$ tokens.

### 2.1 Parameters

We selected the following set of parameters for investigation, all of which are fundamental to vector space model construction[1].

[1]Another obvious parameter would be dimensionality reduction, which we chose not to include because it does not represent a fundamental aspect of VSM construction: dimensionality reduction relies on some original non-reduced model, and directly depends on its quality.

**Vector size** Each component of a vector represents a context (or perhaps more accurately a "contextual element", such as second word to the left of the target word).[2] The number of components varies hugely in the literature, but a typical value is in the low thousands. Here we consider vector sizes ranging from 50,000 to 500,000, to see whether larger vectors lead to better performance.

**Context** There are two main approaches to modelling context: window-based and dependency-based. For window-based methods, contexts are determined by word co-occurrences within a window of a given size, where the window simply spans a number of words occurring around instances of a target word. For dependency-based methods, the contexts are determined by word co-occurrences in a particular syntactic relation with a target word (e.g. target word *dog* is the subject of *run*, where *run*_subj is the context). We consider different window sizes and compare window-based and dependency-based methods.

**Feature granularity** Context words, or "features", are often stemmed or lemmatised. We investigate the effect of stemming and lemmatisation, in particular to see whether the effect varies with corpus size. We also consider more fine-grained features in which each context word is paired with a POS tag or a lexical category from CCG (Steedman, 2000).

**Similarity metric** A variety of metrics can be used to calculate the similarity between two vectors. We consider the similarity metrics in Table 2.

**Weighting** Weighting schemes increase the importance of contexts that are more indicative of the meaning of the target word: the fact that *cat* co-occurs with *purr* is much more informative than its co-occurrence with *the*. Table 3 gives definitions of the weighting schemes considered.

**Stopwords, high frequency cut-off** Function words and stopwords are often considered too uninformative to be suitable context words. Ignoring them not only leads to a reduction in model size and computational effort, but also to a more informative distributional vector. Hence we followed standard practice and did not use stopwords as context words (using the stoplist in NLTK (Bird et al., 2009)). The question we investigated is

[2]We will use the term "feature" or "context" or "context word" to refer to contextual elements.

| Measure | Definition |
|---|---|
| Euclidean | $\frac{1}{1+\sqrt{\sum_{i=1}^{n}(u_i-v_i)^2}}$ |
| Cityblock | $\frac{1}{1+\sum_{i=1}^{n}\lvert u_i-v_i\rvert}$ |
| Chebyshev | $\frac{1}{1+\max_i \lvert u_i-v_i\rvert}$ |
| Cosine | $\frac{u \cdot v}{\lvert u\rvert \lvert v\rvert}$ |
| Correlation | $\frac{(u-\mu_u)\cdot(v-\mu_v)}{\lvert u\rvert \lvert v\rvert}$ |
| Dice | $\frac{2\sum_{i=0}^{n} min(u_i,v_i)}{\sum_{i=0}^{n} u_i+v_i}$ |
| Jaccard | $\frac{u \cdot v}{\sum_{i=0}^{n} u_i+v_i}$ |
| Jaccard2 | $\frac{\sum_{i=0}^{n} min(u_i,v_i)}{\sum_{i=0}^{n} max(u_i,v_i)}$ |
| Lin | $\frac{\sum_{i=0}^{n} u_i+v_i}{\lvert u\rvert+\lvert v\rvert}$ |
| Tanimoto | $\frac{u \cdot v}{\lvert u\rvert+\lvert v\rvert-u \cdot v}$ |
| Jensen-Shannon Div | $1-\frac{\frac{1}{2}(D(u\lvert\rvert\frac{u+v}{2})+D(v\lvert\rvert\frac{u+v}{2}))}{\sqrt{2\log 2}}$ |
| $\alpha$-skew | $1-\frac{D(u\lvert\rvert\alpha v+(1-\alpha)u)}{\sqrt{2\log 2}}$ |

Table 2: Similarity measures between vectors $v$ and $u$, where $v_i$ is the $i$th component of $v$

whether removing more context words, based on a frequency cut-off, can improve performance.

## 3 Experiments

The parameter space is too large to analyse exhaustively, and so we adopted a strategy for how to navigate through it, selecting certain parameters to investigate first, which then get fixed or "clamped" in the remaining experiments. Unless specified otherwise, vectors are generated with the following restrictions and transformations on features: stopwords are removed, numbers mapped to 'NUM', and only strings consisting of alphanumeric characters are allowed. In all experiments, the features consist of the frequency-ranked first $n$ words in the given source corpus.

Four of the five similarity datasets (RG, MC, W353, MEN) contain continuous scales of similarity ratings for word pairs; hence we follow standard practice in using a Spearman correlation coefficient $\rho_s$ for evaluation. The fifth dataset (TOEFL) is a set of multiple-choice questions, for which an accuracy measure is appropriate. Calculating an aggregate score over all datasets is non-trivial, since taking the mean of correlation scores leads to an under-estimation of performance; hence for the aggregate score we use the Fisher-transformed $z$-variable of the correlation datasets, and take the weighted average of its inverse over the correlation datasets and the TOEFL accuracy score (Silver and Dunlap, 1987).

| Scheme | Definition |
|---|---|
| None | $w_{ij} = f_{ij}$ |
| TF-IDF | $w_{ij} = \log(f_{ij}) \times \log(\frac{N}{n_j})$ |
| TF-ICF | $w_{ij} = \log(f_{ij}) \times \log(\frac{N}{f_j})$ |
| Okapi BM25 | $w_{ij} = \frac{f_{ij}}{0.5+1.5\times\frac{f_j}{\frac{f_j}{j}}+f_{ij}} \log\frac{N-n_j+0.5}{f_{ij}+0.5}$ |
| ATC | $w_{ij} = \frac{(0.5+0.5\times\frac{f_{ij}}{max_f})\log(\frac{N}{n_j})}{\sqrt{\sum_{i=1}^{N}[(0.5+0.5\times\frac{f_{ij}}{max_f})\log(\frac{N}{n_j})]^2}}$ |
| LTU | $w_{ij} = \frac{(\log(f_{ij})+1.0)\log(\frac{N}{n_j})}{0.8+0.2\times f_j\times\frac{j}{f_j}}$ |
| MI | $w_{ij} = \log\frac{P(t_{ij}\lvert c_j)}{P(t_{ij})P(c_j)}$ |
| PosMI | $\max(0, \mathrm{MI})$ |
| T-Test | $w_{ij} = \frac{P(t_{ij}\lvert c_j)-P(t_{ij})P(c_j)}{\sqrt{P(t_{ij})P(c_j)}}$ |
| $\chi^2$ | see (Curran, 2004, p. 83) |
| Lin98a | $w_{ij} = \frac{f_{ij}\times f}{f_i\times f_j}$ |
| Lin98b | $w_{ij} = -1\times\log\frac{n_j}{N}$ |
| Gref94 | $w_{ij} = \frac{\log f_{ij}+1}{\log n_j+1}$ |

Table 3: Term weighting schemes. $f_{ij}$ denotes the target word frequency in a particular context, $f_i$ the total target word frequency, $f_j$ the total context frequency, $N$ the total of all frequencies, $n_j$ the number of non-zero contexts. $P(t_{ij}|c_j)$ is defined as $\frac{f_{ij}}{f_j}$ and $P(t_{ij})$ as $\frac{f_{ij}}{N}$.

### 3.1 Vector size

The first parameter we investigate is vector size, measured by the number of features. Vectors are constructed from the BNC using a window-based method, with a window size of 5 (2 words either side of the target word). We experiment with vector sizes up to 0.5M features, which is close to the total number of context words present in the entire BNC according to our preprocessing scheme. Features are added according to frequency in the BNC, with increasingly more rare features being added. For weighting we consider both Positive Mutual Information and T-Test, which have been found to work best in previous research (Bullinaria and Levy, 2012; Curran, 2004). Similarity is computed using Cosine.

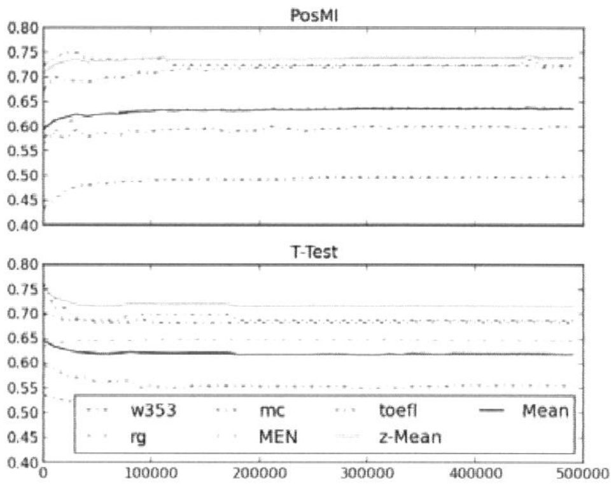


Figure 1: Impact of vector size on performance across different datasets

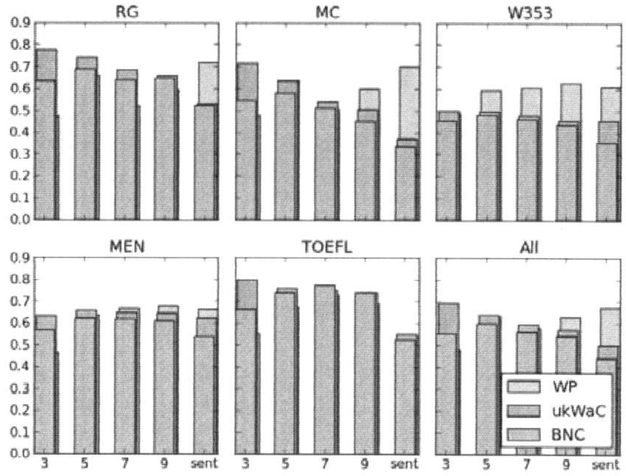


Figure 2: Impact of window size across three corpora

The results in Figure 1 show a clear trend: for both weighting schemes, performance no longer improves after around 50,000 features; in fact, for T-test weighting, and some of the datasets, performance initially declines with an increase in features. Hence we conclude that continuing to add more rare features is detrimental to performance, and that 50,000 features or less will give good performance. An added benefit of smaller vectors is the reduction in computational cost.

### 3.2 Window size

Recent studies have found that the best window size depends on the task at hand. For example, Hill et al. (2013) found that smaller windows work best for measuring similarity of concrete nouns, whereas larger window sizes work better for abstract nouns. Schulte im Walde et al. (2013) found that a large window size worked best for a compositionality dataset of German noun-noun compounds. Similar relations between window size and performance have been found for similar versus related words, as well as for similar versus associated words (Turney and Pantel, 2010).

We experiment with window sizes of 3, 5, 7, 9 and a full sentence. (A window size of $n$ implies $\frac{n-1}{2}$ words either side of the target word.) We use Positive Mutual Information weighting, Cosine similarity, and vectors of size 50,000 (based on the results from Section 3.1). Figure 2 shows the results for all the similarity datasets, with the aggregated score at the bottom right.

Performance was evaluated on three corpora, in order to answer three questions: Does window size affect performance? Does corpus size interact with window size? Does corpus sub-spacing interact with window size? Figure 2 clearly shows the answer to all three questions is "yes". First, ukWaC consistently outperforms the BNC, across all window sizes, indicating that a larger source corpus leads to better performance. Second, we see that the larger ukWaC performs better with smaller window sizes compared to the BNC, with the best ukWaC performance typically being found with a window size of only 3. For the BNC, it appears that a larger window is able to offset the smaller size of corpus to some extent.

We also evaluated on a sub-spaced Wikipedia source corpus similar to Stone et al. (2008), which performs much better with larger window sizes than the BNC or ukWaC. Our explanation for this result is that sub-spacing, resulting from searching for Wikipedia pages with the appropriate target terms, provides a focused, less noisy corpus in which context words some distance from the target word are still relevant to its meaning.

In summary, the highest score is typically achieved with the largest source corpora and smallest window size, with the exception of the much smaller sub-spaced Wikipedia corpus.

### 3.3 Context

The notion of context plays a key role in VSMs. Pado and Lapata (2007) present a comparison of window-based versus dependency-based methods and conclude that dependency-based contexts give better results. We also compare window-based and dependency-based models.

Dependency-parsed versions of the BNC and ukWaC were used to construct syntactically-informed vectors, with a single, labelled arc be-

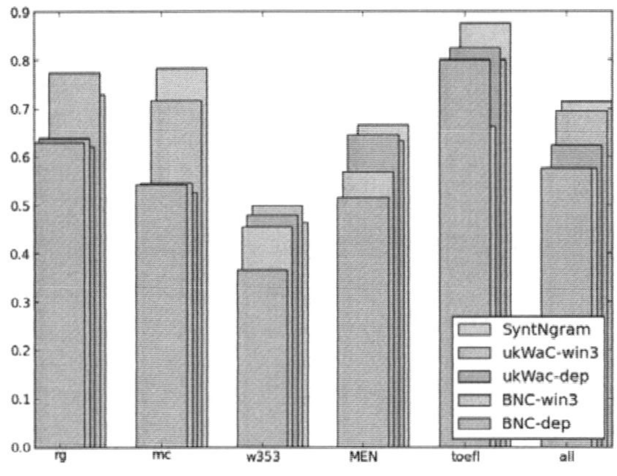


Figure 3: Window versus dependency contexts

tween the target word and context word.[3] Since this effectively provides a window size of 3, we also use a window size of 3 for the window-based method (which provided the best results in Section 3.2 with the ukWaC corpus). As well as the ukWaC and BNC source corpora, we use the Google syntactic N-gram corpus (Goldberg and Orwant, 2013), which is one of the largest corpora to date, and which consists of syntactic n-grams as opposed to window-based n-grams. We use vectors of size 50,000 with Positive Mutual Information weighting and Cosine similarity. Due to its size and associated computational cost, we used only 10,000 contexts for the vectors generated from the syntactic N-gram corpus. The results are shown in Figure 3.

In contrast to the idea that dependency-based methods outperform window-based methods, we find that the window-based models outperform dependency-based models when they are constructed from the same corpus using the small window size. However, Google's syntactic N-gram corpus does indeed outperform window-based methods, even though smaller vectors were used for the Google models (10,000 vs. 50,000 features). We observe large variations across datasets, with window-based methods performing particularly well on some, but not all. In particular, window-based methods clearly outperform dependency-based methods on the RG dataset (for the same source corpus), whereas the opposite trend is observed for the TOEFL synonym dataset. The summary is that the model built from the syntactic N-grams is the overall winner, but when we compare both methods on the same corpus, the window-based method on a large corpus appears to work best (given the small window size).

### 3.4 Feature granularity

Stemming and lemmatisation are standard techniques in NLP and IR to reduce data sparsity. However, with large enough corpora it may be that the loss of information through generalisation hurts performance. In fact, it may be that increased granularity – through the use of grammatical tags – can lead to improved performance. We test these hypotheses by comparing four types of processed context words: lemmatised, stemmed, POS-tagged, and tagged with CCG lexical categories (which can be thought of as fine-grained POS tags (Clark and Curran, 2007)).[4] The source corpora are BNC and ukWaC, using a window-based method with windows of size 5, Positive Mutual Information weighting, vectors of size 50,000 and Cosine similarity. The results are reported in Figure 4.

The ukWaC-generated vectors outperform the BNC-generated ones on all but a single instance for each of the granularities. Stemming yields the best overall performance, and increasing the granularity does not lead to better results. Even with a very large corpus like ukWaC, stemming yields signficantly better results than not reducing the feature granularity at all. Conversely, apart from the results on the TOEFL synonym dataset, increasing the feature granularity of contexts by including POS tags or CCG categories does not yield any improvement.

### 3.5 Similarity-weighting combination

There is contrasting evidence in the literature regarding which combination of similarity metric and weighting scheme works best. Here we investigate this question using vectors of size 50,000, no processing of the context features (i.e., "normal" feature granularity), and a window-based method with a window size of 5. Aggregated scores across the datasets are reported in Tables 4 and 5 for the BNC and ukWaC, respectively.

There are some clear messages to be taken from these large tables of results. First, two weighting schemes perform better than the others: Positive Mutual Information (PosMI) and T-Test. On the BNC, the former yields the best results. There are

[3]The Clark and Curran (2007) parser was used to provide the dependencies.

[4]Using NLTK's Porter stemmer and WordNet lemmatiser.

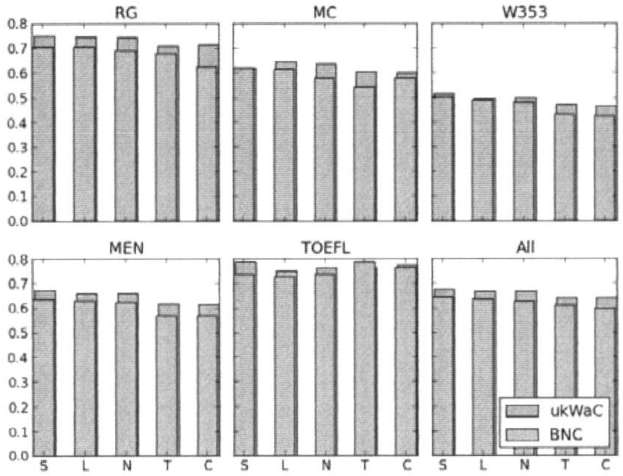


Figure 4: Feature granularity: stemmed (S), lemmatised (L), normal (N), POS-tagged (T) and CCG-tagged (C)

| | RG | MC | W353 | MEN | TOEFL |
|---|---|---|---|---|---|
| P+COS | 0.74 | 0.64 | 0.50 | 0.66 | 0.76 |
| P+COR | 0.74 | 0.65 | **0.58** | **0.71** | **0.83** |
| T+COS | 0.78 | 0.69 | 0.54 | 0.68 | 0.78 |
| T+COR | **0.78** | **0.71** | 0.54 | 0.68 | 0.78 |

Table 6: Similarity scores on individual datasets for positive mutual information (P) and T-test (T) weighting, with cosine (COS) and correlation (COR) similarity

three similarity metrics that perform particularly well: Cosine, Correlation and the Tanimoto coefficient (the latter also being similar to Cosine; see Table 2). The Correlation similarity metric has the most consistent performance across the different weighting schemes, and yields the highest score for both corpora. The most consistent weighting scheme across the two source corpora and similarity metrics appears to be PosMI.

The highest combined aggregate score is that of PosMI with the Correlation metric, in line with the conclusion of Bullinaria and Levy (2012) that PosMI is the best weighting scheme[5]. However, for the large ukWaC corpus, T-Test achieves similarly high aggregate scores, in line with the work of Curran (2004). When we look at these two weighting schemes in more detail, we see that T-Test works best for the RG and MC datasets, while PosMI works best for the others; see Table 6. Correlation is the best similarity metric in all cases.

[5]In some cases, the combination of weighting scheme and similarity metric results in a division by zero or leads to taking the logarithm of a negative number, in which cases we report the aggregate scores as nan (not-a-number).

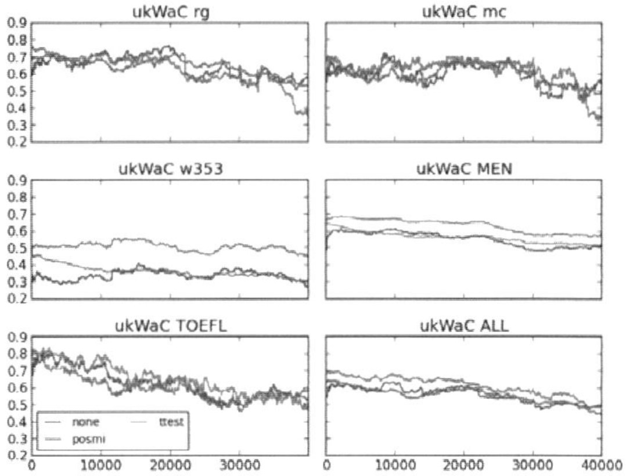


Figure 5: Finding the optimal "contiguous subvector" of size 10,000

### 3.6 Optimal subvector

Stopwords are typically removed from vectors and not used as features. However, Bullinaria and Levy (2012) find that removing stopwords has no effect on performance. A possible explanation is that, since they are using a weighting scheme, the weights of stopwords are low enough that they have effectively been removed anyhow. This raises the question: are we removing stopwords because they contribute little towards the meaning of the target word, or are we removing them because they have high frequency?

The experiment used ukWaC, with a window-based method and window size of 5, normal feature granularity, Cosine similarity and a sliding vector of size 10,000. Having a sliding vector implies that we throw away up to the first 40,000 contexts as we slide across to the 50,000 mark (replacing the higher frequency contexts with lower frequency ones). In effect, we are trying to find the cut-off point where the 10,000-component "contiguous subvector" of the target word vector is optimal (where the features are ordered by frequency). Results are given for PosMI, T-Test and no weighting at all.

The results are shown in Figure 5. T-test outperforms PosMI at the higher frequency ranges (to the left of the plots) but PosMI gives better results for some of the datasets further to the right. For both weighting schemes the performance decreases as high frequency contexts are replaced with lower frequency contexts.

A different picture emerges when no weighting is used, however. Here the performance can *increase* as high-frequency contexts are replaced

| | British National Corpus | | | | | | | | | | | |
|---|---|---|---|---|---|---|---|---|---|---|---|---|
| | COS | COR | DIC | JC1 | JC2 | TAN | LIN | EUC | CIB | CHS | JSD | ASK |
| none | 0.49 | 0.50 | 0.34 | 0.35 | 0.27 | 0.22 | 0.30 | 0.09 | 0.11 | 0.08 | 0.45 | 0.36 |
| tfidf | 0.43 | 0.44 | 0.33 | 0.34 | 0.22 | 0.16 | 0.27 | 0.13 | 0.12 | 0.16 | 0.38 | 0.32 |
| tficf | 0.47 | 0.48 | 0.34 | 0.36 | 0.23 | 0.16 | 0.27 | 0.13 | 0.12 | 0.15 | 0.40 | 0.33 |
| okapi | 0.40 | 0.42 | 0.37 | 0.42 | 0.22 | 0.23 | 0.26 | 0.25 | 0.15 | 0.14 | 0.37 | 0.26 |
| atc | 0.40 | 0.43 | 0.25 | 0.24 | 0.16 | 0.34 | 0.30 | 0.10 | 0.13 | 0.08 | 0.33 | 0.23 |
| ltu | 0.44 | 0.45 | 0.35 | 0.36 | 0.22 | 0.23 | 0.26 | 0.22 | 0.13 | 0.21 | 0.37 | 0.27 |
| mi | 0.58 | 0.61 | 0.31 | 0.56 | 0.29 | -0.07 | 0.45 | 0.15 | 0.10 | 0.09 | 0.16 | -0.04 |
| posmi | 0.63 | 0.66 | 0.52 | 0.58 | 0.35 | -0.08 | 0.45 | 0.15 | 0.11 | 0.06 | 0.54 | 0.46 |
| ttest | 0.63 | 0.62 | 0.11 | 0.34 | 0.08 | 0.63 | 0.17 | 0.18 | 0.14 | 0.11 | nan | nan |
| chisquared | 0.50 | 0.50 | 0.46 | 0.42 | 0.42 | 0.42 | nan | 0.06 | 0.07 | 0.08 | 0.57 | 0.52 |
| lin98b | 0.47 | 0.52 | 0.35 | 0.40 | 0.21 | -0.10 | 0.29 | 0.10 | 0.11 | nan | 0.38 | 0.29 |
| gref94 | 0.46 | 0.49 | 0.35 | 0.37 | 0.23 | 0.06 | 0.28 | 0.12 | 0.11 | 0.09 | 0.41 | 0.30 |

Table 4: Aggregated scores for combinations of weighting schemes and similarity metrics using the BNC. The similarity metrics are Cosine (COS), Correlation (COR), Dice (DIC), Jaccard (JC1), Jaccard2 (JC2), Tanimoto (TAN), Lin (LIN), Euclidean (EUC), CityBlock (CIB), Chebyshev (CHS), Jensen-Shannon Divergence (JSD) and $\alpha$-skew (ASK)

| | ukWaC | | | | | | | | | | | |
|---|---|---|---|---|---|---|---|---|---|---|---|---|
| | COS | COR | DIC | JC1 | JC2 | TAN | LIN | EUC | CIB | CHS | JSD | ASK |
| none | 0.55 | 0.55 | 0.28 | 0.35 | 0.24 | 0.41 | 0.31 | 0.06 | 0.09 | 0.08 | 0.56 | 0.49 |
| tfidf | 0.45 | 0.47 | 0.26 | 0.30 | 0.20 | 0.28 | 0.22 | 0.14 | 0.12 | 0.16 | 0.37 | 0.27 |
| tficf | 0.45 | 0.49 | 0.27 | 0.33 | 0.20 | 0.29 | 0.24 | 0.13 | 0.11 | 0.09 | 0.37 | 0.28 |
| okapi | 0.37 | 0.42 | 0.33 | 0.37 | 0.18 | 0.27 | 0.26 | 0.26 | 0.17 | 0.12 | 0.34 | 0.20 |
| atc | 0.34 | 0.42 | 0.13 | 0.13 | 0.08 | 0.15 | 0.28 | 0.10 | 0.09 | 0.07 | 0.28 | 0.15 |
| ltu | 0.43 | 0.48 | 0.30 | 0.34 | 0.19 | 0.26 | 0.25 | 0.26 | 0.16 | 0.24 | 0.36 | 0.23 |
| mi | 0.51 | 0.53 | 0.18 | 0.51 | 0.16 | 0.28 | 0.37 | 0.18 | 0.10 | 0.09 | 0.12 | nan |
| posmi | 0.67 | 0.70 | 0.56 | 0.62 | 0.42 | 0.59 | 0.52 | 0.23 | 0.15 | 0.06 | 0.60 | 0.49 |
| ttest | 0.70 | 0.70 | 0.16 | 0.48 | 0.10 | 0.70 | 0.22 | 0.16 | 0.11 | 0.15 | nan | nan |
| chisquared | 0.57 | 0.58 | 0.52 | 0.56 | 0.44 | 0.52 | nan | 0.08 | 0.06 | 0.10 | 0.63 | 0.60 |
| lin98b | 0.43 | 0.63 | 0.31 | 0.37 | 0.20 | 0.23 | 0.26 | 0.09 | 0.10 | nan | 0.34 | 0.24 |
| gref94 | 0.48 | 0.54 | 0.27 | 0.33 | 0.20 | 0.17 | 0.23 | 0.13 | 0.11 | 0.09 | 0.38 | 0.25 |

Table 5: Aggregated scores for combinations of weighting schemes and similarity metrics using ukWaC

with lower-frequency ones, with optimal performance comparable to when weighting is used. There are some scenarios where it may be advantageous not to use weighting, for example in an online setting where the total set of vectors is not fixed; in situations where use of a dimensionality reduction technique does not directly allow for weighting, such as random indexing (Sahlgren, 2006); as well as in settings where calculating weights is too expensive. Where to stop the sliding window varies with the datasets, however, and so our conclusion is that the default scheme should be weighting plus high frequency contexts.

## 4 Compositionality

In order to examine whether optimal parameters carry over to vectors that are combined into phrasal vectors using a composition operator, we perform a subset of our experiments on the canonical compositionality dataset from Mitchell and Lapata (2010), using vector addition and pointwise multiplication (the best performing operators in the original study).

We evaluate using two source corpora (the BNC and ukWaC) and two window sizes (small, with a window size of 3; and big, where the full sentence is the window). In addition to the weighting schemes from the previous experiment, we include Mitchell & Lapata's own weighting scheme, which (in our notation) is defined as $w_{ij} = \frac{f_{ij} \times N}{f_i \times f_j}$. While all weighting schemes and similarity metrics were tested, we report only the best performing ones: correlations below 0.5 were ommitted for the sake of brevity. Table 7 shows the results.

We find that many of our findings continue to hold. PosMI and T-Test are the best performing weighting schemes, together with Mitchell & Lapata's own weighting scheme. We find that addition outperforms multiplication (contrary to the original study) and that small window sizes work best, except in the VO case. Performance across corpora is comparable. The best performing similarity metrics are Cosine and Correlation, with the latter having a slight edge over the former.

| | AN | NN | VO | ALL |
|---|---|---|---|---|
| **BNC - Small window** | | | | |
| add-posmi-cosine | 0.57 | 0.56 | 0.52 | 0.55 |
| add-posmi-correlation | **0.66** | **0.60** | 0.53 | **0.60** |
| add-ttest-cosine | 0.59 | 0.54 | 0.53 | 0.56 |
| add-ttest-correlation | 0.60 | 0.54 | 0.53 | 0.56 |
| add-mila-correlation | 0.64 | 0.38 | 0.51 | 0.51 |
| **ukWaC - Small window** | AN | NN | VO | ALL |
| add-posmi-correlation | 0.64 | 0.59 | 0.56 | 0.59 |
| add-ttest-cosine | 0.61 | 0.55 | 0.53 | 0.56 |
| add-ttest-correlation | 0.61 | 0.55 | 0.53 | 0.56 |
| add-mila-correlation | 0.64 | 0.48 | 0.57 | 0.56 |
| mult-mila-correlation | 0.52 | 0.44 | 0.63 | 0.53 |
| **BNC - Large window** | AN | NN | VO | ALL |
| add-posmi-correlation | 0.47 | 0.49 | 0.57 | 0.51 |
| add-ttest-cosine | 0.50 | 0.53 | 0.60 | 0.54 |
| add-ttest-correlation | 0.50 | 0.53 | 0.60 | 0.54 |
| add-mila-correlation | 0.51 | 0.49 | 0.61 | 0.54 |
| mult-posmi-correlation | 0.48 | 0.48 | 0.66 | 0.54 |
| mult-mila-correlation | 0.53 | 0.51 | 0.67 | 0.57 |
| **ukWaC - Large window** | AN | NN | VO | ALL |
| add-posmi-correlation | 0.46 | 0.44 | 0.60 | 0.50 |
| add-ttest-cosine | 0.46 | 0.46 | 0.59 | 0.50 |
| add-ttest-correlation | 0.47 | 0.46 | 0.60 | 0.51 |
| add-mila-correlation | 0.47 | 0.46 | 0.64 | 0.52 |
| mult-posmi-correlation | 0.44 | 0.46 | 0.65 | 0.52 |
| mult-mila-correlation | 0.56 | 0.49 | **0.70** | 0.58 |

Table 7: Selected Spearman $\rho$ scores on the Mitchell & Lapata 2010 compositionality dataset

## 5 Conclusion

Our experiments were designed to investigate a wide range of VSM parameters, using a variety of evaluation tasks and several source corpora. Across each of the experiments, results are competitive with the state of the art. Some important messages can be taken away from this study:

**Experiment 1** Larger vectors do not always lead to better performance. As vector size increases, performance stabilises, and a vector size of around 50,000 appears to be optimal.

**Experiment 2** The size of the window has a clear impact on performance: a large corpus with a small window size performs best, but high performance can be achieved on a small subspaced corpus, if the window size is large.

**Experiment 3** The size of the source corpus is more important than whether the model is window- or dependency-based. Window-based methods with a window size of 3 yield better results than dependency-based methods with a window of 3 (i.e. having a single arc). The Google Syntactic N-gram corpus yields very good performance, but it is unclear whether this is due to being dependency-based or being very large.

**Experiment 4** The granularity of the context words has a relatively low impact on performance, but stemming yields the best results.

**Experiment 5** The optimal combination of weighting scheme and similarity metric is Positive Mutual Information with a mean-adjusted version of Cosine that we have called Correlation. Another high-performing weighting scheme is T-Test, which works better for smaller vector sizes. The Correlation similarity metric consistently outperforms Cosine, and we recommend its use.

**Experiment 6** Use of a weighting scheme obviates the need for removing high-frequency features. Without weighting, many of the high-frequency features should be removed. However, if weighting is an option we recommend its use.

**Compositionality** The best parameters for individual vectors generally carry over to a compositional similarity task where phrasal similarity is evaluated by combining vectors into phrasal vectors.

Furthermore, we observe that in general performance increases as source corpus size increases, so we recommend using a corpus such as ukWaC over smaller corpora like the BNC. Likewise, since the MEN dataset is the largest similarity dataset available and mirrors our aggregate score the best across the various experiments, we recommend evaluating on that similarity task if only a single dataset is used for evaluation.

Obvious extensions include an analysis of the performance of the various dimensionality reduction techniques, examining the importance of window size and feature granularity for dependency-based methods, and further exploring the relation between the size and frequency distribution of a corpus together with the optimal characteristics (such as the high-frequency cut-off point) of vectors generated from that source.

## Acknowledgments

This work has been supported by EPSRC grant EP/I037512/1. We would like to thank Laura Rimell, Tamara Polajnar and Felix Hill for helpful comments and suggestions.

## References


Marco Baroni, Silvia Bernardini, Adriano Ferraresi, and Eros Zanchetta. 2009. The WaCky Wide Web: A collection of very large linguistically processed Web-crawled corpora. *Language Resources and Evaluation*, 43(3):209–226.

Marco Baroni, Raffaella Bernardi, and Roberto Zamparelli. 2013. Frege in Space: A program for compositional distributional semantics. *Linguistic Issues in Language Technologies (LiLT)*.

Steven Bird, Ewan Klein, and Edward Loper. 2009. *Natural Language Processing with Python*. O'Reilly Media.

William Blacoe and Mirella Lapata. 2012. A Comparison of Vector-based Representations for Semantic Composition. In *Proceedings of the 2012 Joint Conference on Empirical Methods in Natural Language Processing and Computational Natural Language Learning*, pages 546–556, Jeju Island, Korea, July. Association for Computational Linguistics.

Elia Bruni, Gemma Boleda, Marco Baroni, and N. K. Tran. 2012. Distributional Semantics in Technicolor. In *Proceedings of the ACL 2012*.

John A. Bullinaria and Joseph P. Levy. 2007. Extracting Semantic Representations from Word Cooccurrence Statistics: A computational study. *Behavior Research Methods*, 39:510–526.

John A. Bullinaria and Joseph P. Levy. 2012. Extracting Semantic Representations from Word Cooccurrence Statistics: Stop-lists, Stemming and SVD. *Behavior Research Methods*, 44:890–907.

L. Burnard. 2007. Reference Guide for the British National Corpus. http://www.natcorp.ox.ac.uk/docs/URG/.

Stephen Clark and James R. Curran. 2007. Wide-Coverage Efficient Statistical Parsing with CCG and Log-Linear Models. *Computational Linguistics*, 33(4):493—552.

Stephen Clark. 2014. Vector Space Models of Lexical Meaning (to appear). In Shalom Lappin and Chris Fox, editors, *Handbook of Contemporary Semantics*. Wiley-Blackwell, Oxford.

James R. Curran and Marc Moens. 2002a. Improvements in Automatic Thesaurus Extraction. In *Proceedings of the ACL-02 workshop on Unsupervised lexical acquisition-Volume 9*, pages 59–66. Association for Computational Linguistics.

James R. Curran and Marc Moens. 2002b. Scaling Context Space. In *Proceedings of the 40th Annual Meeting on Association for Computational Linguistics*, pages 231–238. Association for Computational Linguistics.

James R. Curran. 2004. *From Distributional to Semantic Similarity*. Ph.D. thesis, University of Edinburgh.

Katrin Erk. 2012. Vector Space Models of Word Meaning and Phrase Meaning: A Survey. *Language and Linguistics Compass*, 6(10):635–653.

Lev Finkelstein, Evgeniy Gabrilovich, Yossi Matias, Ehud Rivlin, Zach Solan, Gadi Wolfman, and Eytan Ruppin. 2002. Placing Search in Context: The Concept Revisited. *ACM Transactions on Information Systems*, 20(1):116—131.

Yoav Goldberg and Jon Orwant. 2013. A Dataset of Syntactic-Ngrams over Time from a Very Large Corpus of English Books. In *Second Joint Conference on Lexical and Computational Semantics (*SEM), Volume 1: Proceedings of the Main Conference and the Shared Task: Semantic Textual Similarity*, pages 241–247, Atlanta, Georgia, USA, June. Association for Computational Linguistics.

Gregory Grefenstette. 1994. *Explorations in Automatic Thesaurus Discovery*. Kluwer Academic Publishers, Norwell, MA, USA.

Z. Harris. 1954. Distributional Structure. *Word*, 10(23):146—162.

F. Hill, D. Kiela, and A. Korhonen. 2013. Concreteness and Corpora: A Theoretical and Practical Analysis. In *Proceedings of ACL 2013, Workshop on Cognitive Modelling and Computational Linguistics*, Sofia, Bulgaria.

Thomas K. Landauer and Susan T. Dumais. 1997. A solution to Platos problem: The latent semantic analysis theory of acquisition, induction, and representation of knowledge. *Psychological Review*, 104(2):211–240.

Gabriella Lapesa and Stefan Evert. 2013. Evaluating neighbor rank and distance measures as predictors of semantic priming. In *In Proceedings of the ACL Workshop on Cognitive Modeling and Computational Linguistics (CMCL 2013)*, Sofia, Bulgaria.

G.A. Miller and W.G. Charles. 1991. Contextual Correlates of Semantic Similarity. *Language and Cognitive Processes*, 6(1):1—28.

Jeff Mitchell and Mirella Lapata. 2010. Composition in Distributional Models of Semantics. *Cognitive Science*, 34(8):1388–1429.

Sebastian Pado and Mirella Lapata. 2007. Dependency-based Construction of Semantic Space Models. *Computational Linguistics*, 33(2):161–199.

Douglas L. T. Rohde, Laura M. Gonnerman, and David C. Plaut. 2006. An Improved Model of Semantic Similarity based on Lexical Co-occurence. *Communciations of the ACM*, 8:627–633.

Herbert Rubenstein and John B. Goodenough. 1965. Contextual Correlates of Synonymy. *Commun. ACM*, 8(10):627–633, October.

Magnus Sahlgren. 2006. *The Word-Space Model: Using distributional analysis to represent syntagmatic and paradigmatic relations between words in high-dimensional vector spaces.* Ph.D. thesis, Department of Linguistics, Stockholm University.

Sabine Schulte im Walde, Stefan Müller, and Stephen Roller. 2013. Exploring Vector Space Models to Predict the Compositionality of German Noun-Noun Compounds. In *Proceedings of the 2nd Joint Conference on Lexical and Computational Semantics*, pages 255–265, Atlanta, GA.

N. Clayton Silver and William P. Dunlap. 1987. Averaging Correlation Coefficients: Should Fisher's z Transformation Be Used? *Journal of Applied Psychology*, 72(1):146–148, February.

Mark Steedman. 2000. *The Syntactic Process.* MIT Press, Cambridge, MA, USA.

Benjamin P. Stone, Simon J. Dennis, and Peter J. Kwantes. 2008. A Systematic Comparison of Semantic Models on Human Similarity Rating Data: The Effectiveness of Subspacing. In *The Proceedings of the Thirtieth Conference of the Cognitive Science Society.*

Peter D. Turney and Patrick Pantel. 2010. From Frequency to Meaning: vector space models of semantics. *J. Artif. Int. Res.*, 37(1):141–188, January.

Julie Weeds, David Weir, and Diana McCarthy. 2004. Characterising Measures of Lexical Distributional Similarity. In *Proceedings of Coling 2004*, pages 1015–1021, Geneva, Switzerland, Aug 23–Aug 27. COLING.

S. Zelikovitz and M. Kogan. 2006. Using Web Searches on Important Words to create Background Sets for LSI Classification. In *In Proceedings of the 19th International FLAIRS Conference*, pages 598—603, Menlo Park, CA. AAAI Press.

# Extractive Summarization using Continuous Vector Space Models

**Mikael Kågebäck, Olof Mogren, Nina Tahmasebi, Devdatt Dubhashi**
Computer Science & Engineering
Chalmers University of Technology
SE-412 96, Göteborg
{kageback, mogren, ninat, dubhashi}@chalmers.se

## Abstract

Automatic summarization can help users extract the most important pieces of information from the vast amount of text digitized into electronic form everyday. Central to automatic summarization is the notion of similarity between sentences in text. In this paper we propose the use of continuous vector representations for semantically aware representations of sentences as a basis for measuring similarity. We evaluate different compositions for sentence representation on a standard dataset using the ROUGE evaluation measures. Our experiments show that the evaluated methods improve the performance of a state-of-the-art summarization framework and strongly indicate the benefits of continuous word vector representations for automatic summarization.

## 1 Introduction

The goal of summarization is to capture the important information contained in large volumes of text, and present it in a brief, representative, and consistent summary. A well written summary can significantly reduce the amount of work needed to digest large amounts of text on a given topic. The creation of summaries is currently a task best handled by humans. However, with the explosion of available textual data, it is no longer financially possible, or feasible, to produce all types of summaries by hand. This is especially true if the subject matter has a narrow base of interest, either due to the number of potential readers or the duration during which it is of general interest. A summary describing the events of World War II might for instance be justified to create manually, while a summary of all reviews and comments regarding a certain version of Windows might not. In such cases, automatic summarization is a way forward.

In this paper we introduce a novel application of continuous vector representations to the problem of multi-document summarization. We evaluate different compositions for producing sentence representations based on two different word embeddings on a standard dataset using the ROUGE evaluation measures. Our experiments show that the evaluated methods improve the performance of a state-of-the-art summarization framework which strongly indicate the benefits of continuous word vector representations for this tasks.

## 2 Summarization

There are two major types of automatic summarization techniques, extractive and abstractive. *Extractive summarization* systems create summaries using representative sentences chosen from the input while *abstractive summarization* creates new sentences and is generally considered a more difficult problem.

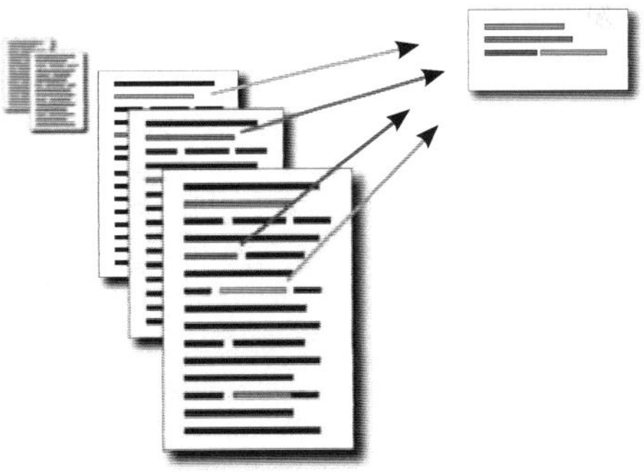

Figure 1: Illustration of Extractive Multi-Document Summarization.

For this paper we consider extractive multi-document summarization, that is, sentences are chosen for inclusion in a summary from a set of documents $D$. Typically, extractive summarization techniques can be divided into two components, the summarization framework and the similarity measures used to compare sentences. Next we present the algorithm used for the framework and in Sec. 2.2 we discuss a typical sentence similarity measure, later to be used as a baseline.

### 2.1 Submodular Optimization

Lin and Bilmes (2011) formulated the problem of extractive summarization as an optimization problem using monotone nondecreasing submodular set functions. A submodular function $F$ on the set of sentences $V$ satisfies the following property: for any $A \subseteq B \subseteq V \backslash \{v\}$, $F(A + \{v\}) - F(A) \geq F(B + \{v\}) - F(B)$ where $v \in V$. This is called the diminishing returns property and captures the intuition that adding a sentence to a small set of sentences (i.e., summary) makes a greater contribution than adding a sentence to a larger set. The aim is then to find a summary that maximizes diversity of the sentences and the coverage of the input text. This objective function can be formulated as follows:

$$\mathcal{F}(S) = \mathcal{L}(S) + \lambda \mathcal{R}(S)$$

where $S$ is the summary, $\mathcal{L}(S)$ is the coverage of the input text, $\mathcal{R}(S)$ is a diversity reward function. The $\lambda$ is a trade-off coefficient that allows us to define the importance of coverage versus diversity of the summary. In general, this kind of optimization problem is NP-hard, however, if the objective function is submodular there is a fast scalable algorithm that returns an approximation with a guarantee. In the work of Lin and Bilmes (2011) a simple submodular function is chosen:

$$\mathcal{L}(S) = \sum_{i \in V} \min\{\sum_{j \in S} \mathrm{Sim}(i,j), \alpha \sum_{j \in V} \mathrm{Sim}(i,j)\} \tag{1}$$

The first argument measures similarity between sentence $i$ and the summary $S$, while the second argument measures similarity between sentence $i$ and the rest of the input $V$. $\mathrm{Sim}(i, j)$ is the similarity between sentence $i$ and sentence $j$ and $0 \leq \alpha \leq 1$ is a threshold coefficient. The diversity reward function $\mathcal{R}(S)$ can be found in (Lin and Bilmes, 2011).

### 2.2 Traditional Similarity Measure

Central to most extractive summarization systems is the use of sentence similarity measures ($\mathrm{Sim}(i, j)$ in Eq. 1). Lin and Bilmes measure similarity between sentences by representing each sentence using *tf-idf* (Salton and McGill, 1986) vectors and measuring the cosine angle between vectors. Each sentence is represented by a word vector $\mathbf{w} = (w_1, \ldots, w_N)$ where $N$ is the size of the vocabulary. Weights $w_{ki}$ correspond to the *tf-idf* value of word $k$ in the sentence $i$. The weights $\mathrm{Sim}(i, j)$ used in the $\mathcal{L}$ function in Eq. 1 are found using the following similarity measure.

$$\mathrm{Sim}(i,j) = \frac{\sum\limits_{w \in i} \mathrm{tf}_{w,i} \times \mathrm{tf}_{w,j} \times \mathrm{idf}_w^2}{\sqrt{\sum\limits_{w \in i} \mathrm{tf}_{w,i}^2 \times \mathrm{idf}_w^2} \sqrt{\sum\limits_{w \in j} \mathrm{tf}_{w,j}^2 \times \mathrm{idf}_w^2}} \tag{2}$$

where $\mathrm{tf}_{w,i}$ and $\mathrm{tf}_{w,j}$ are the number of occurrences of $w$ in sentence $i$ and $j$, and $\mathrm{idf}_w$ is the inverse document frequency (*idf*) of $w$.

In order to have a high similarity between sentences using the above measure, two sentences must have an overlap of highly scored *tf-idf* words. The overlap must be exact to count towards the similarity, e.g, the terms *The US President* and *Barack Obama* in different sentences will not add towards the similarity of the sentences. To capture deeper similarity, in this paper we will investigate the use of continuous vector representations for measuring similarity between sentences. In the next sections we will describe the basics needed for creating continuous vector representations and methods used to create sentence representations that can be used to measure sentence similarity.

## 3 Background on Deep Learning

*Deep learning* (Hinton et al., 2006; Bengio, 2009) is a modern interpretation of artificial neural networks (ANN), with an emphasis on deep network architectures. Deep learning can be used for challenging problems like image and speech recognition (Krizhevsky et al., 2012; Graves et al., 2013), as well as language modeling (Mikolov et al., 2010), and in all cases, able to achieve state-of-the-art results.

Inspired by the brain, ANNs use a neuron-like construction as their primary computational unit. The behavior of a neuron is entirely controlled by its input weights. Hence, the weights are where the information learned by the neuron is stored. More precisely the output of a neuron is computed as the weighted sum of its inputs, and squeezed into the interval $[0, 1]$ using a sigmoid function:

$$y_i = g(\theta_i^T \mathbf{x}) \tag{3}$$

$$g(z) = \frac{1}{1 + e^{-z}} \tag{4}$$

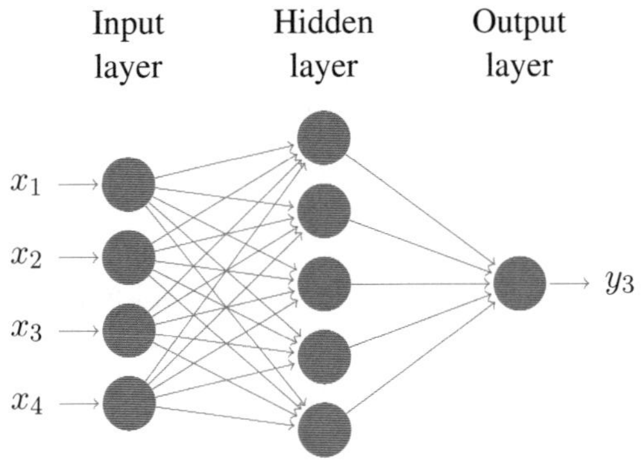


Figure 2: FFNN with four input neurons, one hidden layer, and 1 output neuron. This type of architecture is appropriate for binary classification of some data $\mathbf{x} \in \mathbb{R}^4$, however depending on the complexity of the input, the number and size of the hidden layers should be scaled accordingly.

where $\theta_i$ are the weights associated with neuron $i$ and $\mathbf{x}$ is the input. Here the sigmoid function ($g$) is chosen to be the logistic function, but it may also be modeled using other sigmoid shaped functions, e.g. the hyperbolic tangent function.

The neurons can be organized in many different ways. In some architectures, loops are permitted. These are referred to as *recurrent neural networks*. However, all networks considered here are non-cyclic topologies. In the rest of this section we discuss a few general architectures in more detail, which will later be employed in the evaluated models.

### 3.1 Feed Forward Neural Network

A feed forward neural network (FFNN) (Haykin, 2009) is a type of ANN where the neurons are structured in layers, and only connections to subsequent layers are allowed, see Fig 2. The algorithm is similar to logistic regression using non-linear terms. However, it does not rely on the user to choose the non-linear terms needed to fit the data, making it more adaptable to changing datasets. The first layer in a FFNN is called the input layer, the last layer is called the output layer, and the interim layers are called hidden layers. The hidden layers are optional but necessary to fit complex patterns.

Training is achieved by minimizing the network error ($E$). How $E$ is defined differs between different network architectures, but is in general a differentiable function of the produced output and

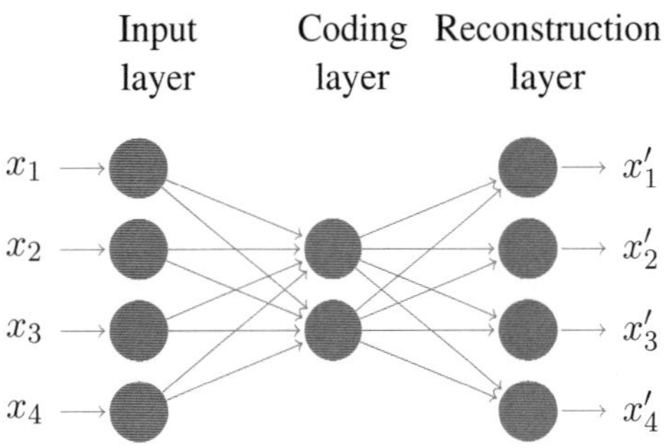


Figure 3: The figure shows an auto-encoder that compresses four dimensional data into a two dimensional code. This is achieved by using a bottleneck layer, referred to as a coding layer.

the expected output. In order to minimize this function the gradient $\frac{\partial E}{\partial \Theta}$ first needs to be calculated, where $\Theta$ is a matrix of all parameters, or weights, in the network. This is achieved using backpropagation (Rumelhart et al., 1986). Secondly, these gradients are used to minimize $E$ using e.g. gradient descent. The result of this processes is a set of weights that enables the network to do the desired input-output mapping, as defined by the training data.

### 3.2 Auto-Encoder

An auto-encoder (AE) (Hinton and Salakhutdinov, 2006), see Fig. 3, is a type of FFNN with a topology designed for dimensionality reduction. The input and the output layers in an AE are identical, and there is at least one hidden bottleneck layer that is referred to as the coding layer. The network is trained to reconstruct the input data, and if it succeeds this implies that all information in the data is necessarily contained in the compressed representation of the coding layer.

A shallow AE, i.e. an AE with no extra hidden layers, will produce a similar code as principal component analysis. However, if more layers are added, before and after the coding layer, non-linear manifolds can be found. This enables the network to compress complex data, with minimal loss of information.

### 3.3 Recursive Neural Network

A recursive neural network (RvNN), see Fig. 4, first presented by Socher et al. (2010), is a type of feed forward neural network that can process data through an arbitrary binary tree structure, e.g. a

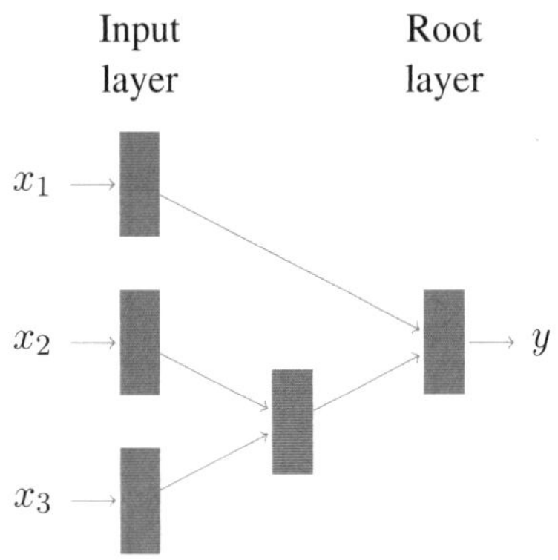


Figure 4: The recursive neural network architecture makes it possible to handle variable length input data. By using the same dimensionality for all layers, arbitrary binary tree structures can be recursively processed.

binary parse tree produced by linguistic parsing of a sentence. This is achieved by enforcing weight constraints across all nodes and restricting the output of each node to have the same dimensionality as its children.

The input data is placed in the leaf nodes of the tree, and the structure of this tree is used to guide the recursion up to the root node. A compressed representation is calculated recursively at each non-terminal node in the tree, using the same weight matrix at each node. More precisely, the following formulas can be used:

$$z_p = \theta_p^T [x_l; x_r] \tag{5a}$$

$$y_p = g(z_p) \tag{5b}$$

where $y_p$ is the computed parent state of neuron $p$, and $z_p$ the induced field for the same neuron. $[x_l; x_r]$ is the concatenation of the state belonging to the right and left sibling nodes. This process results in a fixed length representation for hierarchical data of arbitrary length. Training of the model is done using backpropagation through structure, introduced by Goller and Kuchler (1996).

## 4 Word Embeddings

Continuous distributed vector representation of words, also referred to as word embeddings, was first introduced by Bengio et al. (2003). A word embedding is a continuous vector representation that captures semantic and syntactic information about a word. These representations can be used to unveil dimensions of similarity between words, e.g. singular or plural.

### 4.1 Collobert & Weston

Collobert and Weston (2008) introduce an efficient method for computing word embeddings, in this work referred to as *CW* vectors. This is achieved firstly, by scoring a valid n-gram ($\mathbf{x}$) and a corrupted n-gram ($\bar{\mathbf{x}}$) (where the center word has been randomly chosen), and secondly, by training the network to distinguish between these two n-grams. This is done by minimizing the hinge loss

$$\max(0, 1 - s(\mathbf{x}) + s(\bar{\mathbf{x}})) \tag{6}$$

where $s$ is the scoring function, i.e. the output of a FFNN that maps between the word embeddings of an n-gram to a real valued score. Both the parameters of the scoring function and the word embeddings are learned in parallel using backpropagation.

### 4.2 Continuous Skip-gram

A second method for computing word embeddings is the Continuous Skip-gram model, see Fig. 5, introduced by Mikolov et al. (2013a). This model is used in the implementation of their word embeddings tool *Word2Vec*. The model is trained to predict the context surrounding a given word. This is accomplished by maximizing the objective function

$$\frac{1}{T} \sum_{t=1}^{T} \sum_{-c \leq j \leq c, j \neq 0} \log p(w_{t+j} | w_t) \tag{7}$$

where $T$ is the number of words in the training set, and $c$ is the length of the training context. The probability $p(w_{t+j}|w_t)$ is approximated using the hierarchical softmax introduced by Bengio et al. (2002) and evaluated in a paper by Morin and Bengio (2005).

## 5 Phrase Embeddings

Word embeddings have proven useful in many natural language processing (NLP) tasks. For summarization, however, sentences need to be compared. In this section we present two different methods for deriving phrase embeddings, which in Section 5.3 will be used to compute sentence to sentence similarities.

### 5.1 Vector addition

The simplest way to represent a sentence is to consider it as the sum of all words without regarding word orders. This was considered by

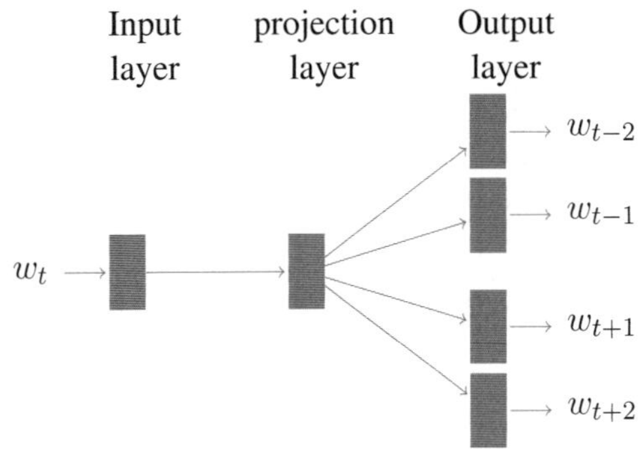


Figure 5: The continuous Skip-gram model. Using the input word ($w_t$) the model tries to predict which words will be in its context ($w_{t \pm c}$).

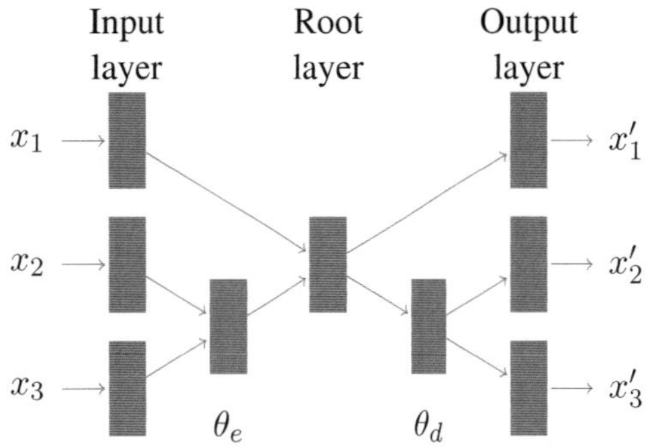


Figure 6: The structure of an unfolding RAE, on a three word phrase ($[x_1, x_2, x_3]$). The weight matrix $\theta_e$ is used to encode the compressed representations, while $\theta_d$ is used to decode the representations and reconstruct the sentence.

Mikolov et al. (2013b) for representing short phrases. The model is expressed by the following equation:

$$\mathbf{x}_p = \sum_{\mathbf{x}_w \in \{\text{sentence}\}} \mathbf{x}_w \tag{8}$$

where $x_p$ is a phrase embedding, and $x_w$ is a word embedding. We use this method for computing phrase embeddings as a baseline in our experiments.

### 5.2 Unfolding Recursive Auto-encoder

The second model is more sophisticated, taking into account also the order of the words and the grammar used. An unfolding recursive auto-encoder (RAE) is used to derive the phrase embedding on the basis of a binary parse tree. The unfolding RAE was introduced by Socher et al. (2011) and uses two RvNNs, one for encoding the compressed representations, and one for decoding them to recover the original sentence, see Figure 6. The network is subsequently trained by minimizing the reconstruction error.

Forward propagation in the network is done by recursively applying Eq. 5a and 5b for each triplet in the tree in two phases. First, starting at the center node (root of the tree) and recursively pulling the data from the input. Second, again starting at the center node, recursively pushing the data towards the output. Backpropagation is done in a similar manner using backpropagation through structure (Goller and Kuchler, 1996).

### 5.3 Measuring Similarity

Phrase embeddings provide semantically aware representations for sentences. For summarization, we need to measure the similarity between two representations and will make use of the following two vector similarity measures. The first similarity measure is the cosine similarity, transformed to the interval of $[0, 1]$

$$\text{Sim}(i, j) = \left( \frac{\mathbf{x}_i^T \mathbf{x}_j}{\|\mathbf{x}_j\| \|\mathbf{x}_j\|} + 1 \right) / 2 \tag{9}$$

where $\mathbf{x}$ denotes a phrase embedding The second similarity is based on the complement of the Euclidean distance and computed as:

$$\text{Sim}(i, j) = 1 - \frac{1}{\max_{k,n} \sqrt{\| \mathbf{x}_k - \mathbf{x}_n \|^2}} \sqrt{\| \mathbf{x}_j - \mathbf{x}_i \|^2} \tag{10}$$

## 6 Experiments

In order to evaluate phrase embeddings for summarization we conduct several experiments and compare different phrase embeddings with *tf-idf* based vectors.

### 6.1 Experimental Settings

Seven different configuration were evaluated. The first configuration provides us with a baseline and is denoted *Original* for the Lin-Bilmes method described in Sec. 2.1. The remaining configurations comprise selected combinations of word embeddings, phrase embeddings, and similarity measures.

The first group of configurations are based on vector addition using both Word2Vec and CW vectors. These vectors are subsequently compared using both cosine similarity and Euclidean distance. The second group of configurations are built upon recursive auto-encoders using CW vectors and are also compared using cosine similarity as well as Euclidean distance.

The methods are named according to: VectorType_EmbeddingMethod$_{SimilarityMethod}$, e.g. W2V_Add$_{Cos}$ for Word2Vec vectors combined using vector addition and compared using cosine similarity.

To get an upper bound for each ROUGE score an exhaustive search were performed, where each possible pair of sentences were evaluated, and maximized w.r.t the ROUGE score.

### 6.2 Dataset and Evaluation

The Opinosis dataset (Ganesan et al., 2010) consists of short user reviews in 51 different topics. Each of these topics contains between 50 and 575 sentences and are a collection of user reviews made by different authors about a certain characteristic of a hotel, car or a product (e.g. *"Location of Holiday Inn, London"* and *"Fonts, Amazon Kindle"*). The dataset is well suited for multi-document summarization (each sentence is considered its own document), and includes between 4 and 5 gold-standard summaries (not sentences chosen from the documents) created by human authors for each topic.

Each summary is evaluated with ROUGE, that works by counting word overlaps between generated summaries and gold standard summaries. Our results include R-1, R-2, and R-SU4, which counts matches in unigrams, bigrams, and skip-bigrams respectively. The skip-bigrams allow four words in between (Lin, 2004).

The measures reported are recall (R), precision (P), and F-score (F), computed for each topic individually and averaged. Recall measures what fraction of a human created gold standard summary that is captured, and precision measures what fraction of the generated summary that is in the gold standard. F-score is a standard way to combine recall and precision, computed as $F = 2\frac{P*R}{P+R}$.

### 6.3 Implementation

All results were obtained by running an implementation of Lin-Bilmes submodular optimization summarizer, as described in Sec. 2.1. Also, we have chosen to fix the length of the summaries to two sentences because the length of the gold-standard summaries are typically around two sentences. The CW vectors used were trained by Turian et al. (2010)[1], and the Word2Vec vectors by Mikolov et al. (2013b)[2]. The unfolding RAE used is based on the implementation by Socher et al. (2011)[3], and the parse trees for guiding the recursion was generated using the Stanford Parser (Klein and Manning, 2003)[4].

### 6.4 Results

The results from the ROUGE evaluation are compiled in Table 1. We find for all measures (recall, precision, and F-score), that the phrase embeddings outperform the original Lin-Bilmes. For recall, we find that CW_Add$_{Cos}$ achieves the highest result, while for precision and F-score the CW_Add$_{Euc}$ perform best. These results are consistent for all versions of ROUGE scores reported (1, 2 and SU4), providing a strong indication for phrase embeddings in the context of automatic summarization.

Unfolding RAE on CW vectors and vector addition on W2V vectors gave comparable results w.r.t. each other, generally performing better than original Linn-Bilmes but not performing as well as vector addition of CW vectors.

The results denoted OPT in Table 1 describe the upper bound score, where each row represents optimal recall and F-score respectively. The best results are achieved for R-1 with a maximum recall of 57.86%. This is a consequence of hand created gold standard summaries used in the evaluation, that is, we cannot achieve full recall or F-score when the sentences in the gold standard summaries are not taken from the underlying documents and thus, they can never be fully matched using extractive summarization. R-2 and SU4 have lower maximum recall and F-score, with 22.9% and 29.5% respectively.

### 6.5 Discussion

The results of this paper show great potential for employing word and phrase embeddings in summarization. We believe that by using embeddings we move towards more semantically aware summarization systems. In the future, we anticipate

[1]http://metaoptimize.com/projects/wordreprs/
[2]https://code.google.com/p/word2vec/
[3]http://nlp.stanford.edu/ socherr/codeRAEVectorsNIPS2011.zip
[4]http://nlp.stanford.edu/software/lex-parser.shtml

Table 1: ROUGE scores for summaries using different similarity measures. OPT constitutes the optimal ROUGE scores on this dataset.

| ROUGE-1 | | | |
|---|---|---|---|
| | **R** | **P** | **F** |
| $OPT_R$ | **57.86** | 21.96 | 30.28 |
| $OPT_F$ | 45.93 | 48.84 | **46.57** |
| $CW\_RAE_{Cos}$ | 27.37 | 19.89 | 22.00 |
| $CW\_RAE_{Euc}$ | 29.25 | 19.77 | 22.62 |
| $CW\_Add_{Cos}$ | **34.72** | 11.75 | 17.16 |
| $CW\_Add_{Euc}$ | 29.12 | **22.75** | **24.88** |
| $W2V\_Add_{Cos}$ | 30.86 | 16.81 | 20.93 |
| $W2V\_Add_{Euc}$ | 28.71 | 16.67 | 20.75 |
| Original | 25.82 | 19.58 | 20.57 |
| **ROUGE-2** | | | |
| | **R** | **P** | **F** |
| $OPT_R$ | **22.96** | 12.31 | 15.33 |
| $OPT_F$ | 20.42 | 19.94 | **19.49** |
| $CW\_RAE_{Cos}$ | 4.68 | 3.18 | 3.58 |
| $CW\_RAE_{Euc}$ | 4.82 | 3.24 | 3.67 |
| $CW\_Add_{Cos}$ | **5.89** | 1.81 | 2.71 |
| $CW\_Add_{Euc}$ | 5.12 | **3.60** | **4.10** |
| $W2V\_Add_{Cos}$ | 5.71 | 3.08 | 3.82 |
| $W2V\_Add_{Euc}$ | 3.86 | 1.95 | 2.54 |
| Original | 3.92 | 2.50 | 2.87 |
| **ROUGE-SU4** | | | |
| | **R** | **P** | **F** |
| $OPT_R$ | **29.50** | 13.53 | 17.70 |
| $OPT_F$ | 23.17 | 26.50 | **23.70** |
| $CW\_RAE_{Cos}$ | 9.61 | 6.23 | 6.95 |
| $CW\_RAE_{Euc}$ | 9.95 | 6.17 | 7.04 |
| $CW\_Add_{Cos}$ | **12.38** | 3.27 | 5.03 |
| $CW\_Add_{Euc}$ | 10.54 | **7.59** | **8.35** |
| $W2V\_Add_{Cos}$ | 11.94 | 5.52 | 7.12 |
| $W2V\_Add_{Euc}$ | 9.78 | 4.69 | 6.15 |
| Original | 9.15 | 6.74 | 6.73 |

improvements for the field of automatic summarization as the quality of the word vectors improve and we find enhanced ways of composing and comparing the vectors.

It is interesting to compare the results of different composition techniques on the CW vectors, where vector addition surprisingly outperforms the considerably more sophisticated unfolding RAE. However, since the unfolding RAE uses syntactic information, this may be a result of using a dataset consisting of low quality text.

In the interest of comparing word embeddings, results using vector addition and cosine similarity were computed based on both CW and Word2Vec vectors. Supported by the achieved results CW vectors seems better suited for sentence similarities in this setting.

An issue we encountered with using precomputed word embeddings was their limited vocabulary, in particular missing uncommon (or common incorrect) spellings. This problem is particularly pronounced on the evaluated Opinosis dataset, since the text is of low quality. Future work is to train word embeddings on a dataset used for summarization to better capture the specific semantics and vocabulary.

The optimal R-1 scores are higher than R-2 and SU4 (see Table 1) most likely because the score ignores word order and considers each sentence as a set of words. We come closest to the optimal score for R-1, where we achieve 60% of maximal recall and 49% of F-score. Future work is to investigate why we achieve a much lower recall and F-score for the other ROUGE scores.

Our results suggest that the phrase embeddings capture the kind of information that is needed for the summarization task. The embeddings are the underpinnings of the decisions on which sentences that are representative of the whole input text, and which sentences that would be redundant when combined in a summary. However, the fact that we at most achieve 60% of maximal recall suggests that the phrase embeddings are not complete w.r.t summarization and might benefit from being combined with other similarity measures that can capture complementary information, for example using multiple kernel learning.

## 7 Related Work

To the best of our knowledge, continuous vector space models have not previously been used in summarization tasks. Therefore, we split this section in two, handling summarization and continuous vector space models separately.

### 7.1 Continuous Vector Space Models

Continuous distributed vector representation of words was first introduced by Bengio et al. (2003).

They employ a FFNN, using a window of words as input, and train the model to predict the next word. This is computed using a big softmax layer that calculate the probabilities for each word in the vocabulary. This type of exhaustive estimation is necessary in some NLP applications, but makes the model heavy to train.

If the sole purpose of the model is to derive word embeddings this can be exploited by using a much lighter output layer. This was suggested by Collobert and Weston (2008), which swapped the heavy softmax against a hinge loss function. The model works by scoring a set of consecutive words, distorting one of the words, scoring the distorted set, and finally training the network to give the correct set a higher score.

Taking the lighter concept even further, Mikolov et al. (2013a) introduced a model called Continuous Skip-gram. This model is trained to predict the context surrounding a given word using a shallow neural network. The model is less aware of the order of words, than the previously mentioned models, but can be trained efficiently on considerably larger datasets.

An early attempt at merging word representations into representations for phrases and sentences is introduced by Socher et al. (2010). The authors present a recursive neural network architecture (RvNN) that is able to jointly learn parsing and phrase/sentence representation. Though not able to achieve state-of-the-art results, the method provides an interesting path forward. The model uses one neural network to derive all merged representations, applied recursively in a binary parse tree. This makes the model fast and easy to train but requires labeled data for training.

### 7.2 Summarization Techniques

Radev et al. (2004) pioneered the use of cluster centroids in their work with the idea to group, in the same cluster, those sentences which are highly similar to each other, thus generating a number of clusters. To measure the similarity between a pair of sentences, the authors use the cosine similarity measure where sentences are represented as weighted vectors of *tf-idf* terms. Once sentences are clustered, sentence selection is performed by selecting a subset of sentences from each cluster.

In TextRank (2004), a document is represented as a graph where each sentence is denoted by a vertex and pairwise similarities between sentences are represented by edges with a weight corresponding to the similarity between the sentences. The Google PageRank ranking algorithm is used to estimate the importance of different sentences and the most important sentences are chosen for inclusion in the summary.

Bonzanini, Martinez, Roelleke (2013) presented an algorithm that starts with the set of all sentences in the summary and then iteratively chooses sentences that are unimportant and removes them. The sentence removal algorithm obtained good results on the Opinosis dataset, in particular w.r.t F-scores.

We have chosen to compare our work with that of Lin and Bilmes (2011), described in Sec. 2.1. Future work is to make an exhaustive comparison using a larger set similarity measures and summarization frameworks.

## 8 Conclusions

We investigated the effects of using phrase embeddings for summarization, and showed that these can significantly improve the performance of the state-of-the-art summarization method introduced by Lin and Bilmes in (2011). Two implementations of word vectors and two different approaches for composition where evaluated. All investigated combinations improved the original Lin-Bilmes approach (using *tf-idf* representations of sentences) for at least two ROUGE scores, and top results where found using vector addition on CW vectors.

In order to further investigate the applicability of continuous vector representations for summarization, in future work we plan to try other summarization methods. In particular we will use a method based on multiple kernel learning were phrase embeddings can be combined with other similarity measures. Furthermore, we aim to use a novel method for sentence representation similar to the RAE using multiplicative connections controlled by the local context in the sentence.

## Acknowledgments

The authors would like to acknowledge the project *Towards a knowledge-based culturomics* supported by a framework grant from the Swedish Research Council (2012–2016; dnr 2012-5738), and the project *Data-driven secure business intelligence* grant IIS11-0089 from the Swedish Foundation for Strategic Research (SSF).

## References


Yoshua Bengio, Réjean Ducharme, Pascal Vincent, and Christian Jauvin. 2003. A neural probabilistic language model. *Journal of Machine Learning Research*, 3:1137–1155.

Yoshua Bengio. 2002. New distributed probabilistic language models. Technical Report 1215, Département d'informatique et recherche opérationnelle, Université de Montréal.

Yoshua Bengio. 2009. Learning deep architectures for ai. *Foundations and trends® in Machine Learning*, 2(1):1–127.

Marco Bonzanini, Miguel Martinez-Alvarez, and Thomas Roelleke. 2013. Extractive summarisation via sentence removal: Condensing relevant sentences into a short summary. In *Proceedings of the 36th International ACM SIGIR Conference on Research and Development in Information Retrieval*, SIGIR '13, pages 893–896. ACM.

Ronan Collobert and Jason Weston. 2008. A unified architecture for natural language processing: Deep neural networks with multitask learning. In *Proceedings of the 25th international conference on Machine learning*, pages 160–167. ACM.

Kavita Ganesan, ChengXiang Zhai, and Jiawei Han. 2010. Opinosis: a graph-based approach to abstractive summarization of highly redundant opinions. In *Proceedings of the 23rd International Conference on Computational Linguistics*, pages 340–348. ACL.

Christoph Goller and Andreas Kuchler. 1996. Learning task-dependent distributed representations by backpropagation through structure. In *IEEE International Conference on Neural Networks*, volume 1, pages 347–352. IEEE.

Alex Graves, Abdel-rahman Mohamed, and Geoffrey Hinton. 2013. Speech recognition with deep recurrent neural networks. *arXiv preprint arXiv:1303.5778.*

S.S. Haykin. 2009. *Neural Networks and Learning Machines.* Number v. 10 in Neural networks and learning machines. Prentice Hall.

Geoffrey E Hinton and Ruslan R Salakhutdinov. 2006. Reducing the dimensionality of data with neural networks. *Science*, 313(5786):504–507.

Geoffrey E Hinton, Simon Osindero, and Yee-Whye Teh. 2006. A fast learning algorithm for deep belief nets. *Neural computation*, 18(7):1527–1554.

Dan Klein and Christopher D Manning. 2003. Fast exact inference with a factored model for natural language parsing. *Advances in neural information processing systems*, pages 3–10.

Alex Krizhevsky, Ilya Sutskever, and Geoff Hinton. 2012. Imagenet classification with deep convolutional neural networks. In *Advances in Neural Information Processing Systems 25*, pages 1106–1114.

Hui Lin and Jeff Bilmes. 2011. A class of submodular functions for document summarization. In *Proceedings of the 49th Annual Meeting of the Association for Computational Linguistics: Human Language Technologies*, pages 510–520. ACL.

Chin-Yew Lin. 2004. Rouge: A package for automatic evaluation of summaries. In *Text Summarization Branches Out: Proceedings of the ACL-04 Workshop*, pages 74–81.

Rada Mihalcea and Paul Tarau. 2004. TextRank: Bringing order into texts. In *Proceedings of EMNLP*, volume 4. Barcelona, Spain.

Tomas Mikolov, Martin Karafiát, Lukas Burget, Jan Cernockỳ, and Sanjeev Khudanpur. 2010. Recurrent neural network based language model. In *INTERSPEECH*, pages 1045–1048.

Tomas Mikolov, Kai Chen, Greg Corrado, and Jeffrey Dean. 2013a. Efficient estimation of word representations in vector space. *ArXiv preprint arXiv:1301.3781.*

Tomas Mikolov, Ilya Sutskever, Kai Chen, Greg S Corrado, and Jeff Dean. 2013b. Distributed representations of words and phrases and their compositionality. In *Advances in Neural Information Processing Systems*, pages 3111–3119.

Frederic Morin and Yoshua Bengio. 2005. Hierarchical probabilistic neural network language model. In *AISTATS'05*, pages 246–252.

Dragomir R Radev, Hongyan Jing, Małgorzata Styś, and Daniel Tam. 2004. Centroid-based summarization of multiple documents. *Information Processing & Management*, 40(6):919–938.

David E Rumelhart, Geoffrey E Hinton, and Ronald J Williams. 1986. Learning representations by backpropagating errors. *Nature*, 323(6088):533–536.

Gerard Salton and Michael J. McGill. 1986. *Introduction to Modern Information Retrieval.* McGraw-Hill, Inc., New York, NY, USA.

Richard Socher, Christopher D Manning, and Andrew Y Ng. 2010. Learning continuous phrase representations and syntactic parsing with recursive neural networks. In *Proceedings of the NIPS-2010 Deep Learning and Unsupervised Feature Learning Workshop.*

Richard Socher, Eric H. Huang, Jeffrey Pennington, Andrew Y. Ng, and Christopher D. Manning. 2011. Dynamic Pooling and Unfolding Recursive Autoencoders for Paraphrase Detection. In *Advances in Neural Information Processing Systems 24.*

Joseph Turian, Lev Ratinov, and Yoshua Bengio. 2010. Word representations: a simple and general method for semi-supervised learning. In *Proceedings of the 48th Annual Meeting of the Association for Computational Linguistics*, pages 384–394. ACL.

# Investigating the Contribution of Distributional Semantic Information for Dialogue Act Classification

**Dmitrijs Milajevs**
Queen Mary University of London
d.milajevs@qmul.ac.uk

**Matthew Purver**
Queen Mary University of London
m.purver@qmul.ac.uk

## Abstract

This paper presents a series of experiments in applying compositional distributional semantic models to dialogue act classification. In contrast to the widely used bag-of-words approach, we build the meaning of an utterance from its parts by composing the distributional word vectors using vector addition and multiplication. We investigate the contribution of word sequence, dialogue act sequence, and distributional information to the performance, and compare with the current state of the art approaches. Our experiment suggests that that distributional information is useful for dialogue act tagging but that simple models of compositionality fail to capture crucial information from word and utterance sequence; more advanced approaches (e.g. sequence- or grammar-driven, such as categorical, word vector composition) are required.

## 1 Introduction

One of the fundamental tasks in automatic dialogue processing is dialogue act tagging: labelling each utterance with a tag relating to its function in the dialogue and effect on the emerging context: *greeting*, *query*, *statement* etc (see e.g. (Core, 1998)). Although factors such as intonation also play a role (see e.g. (Jurafsky et al., 1998)), one of the most important sources of information in this task is the semantic meaning of an utterance, and this is reflected in the fact that people use similar words when they perform similar utterance acts. For example, utterances which state opinion (tagged `sv` in the standard DAMSL schema, see below) often include words such as "*I think*", "*I believe*", "*I guess*" etc. Hence, a similarity-based model of meaning — for instance, a distributional semantic model — should provide benefits over a purely word-based model for dialogue act tagging. However, since utterances generally consist of more than one word, one has to be able to extend such similarity-based models from single words to sentences and/or complete utterances. Hence, we consider here the application of compositional distributional semantics for this task.

Here, we extend bag-of-word models common in previous approaches (Serafin et al., 2003) with simple compositional distributional operations (Mitchell and Lapata, 2008) and examine the improvements gained. These improvements suggest that distributional information does improve performance, but that more sophisticated compositional operations such as matrix multiplication (Baroni and Zamparelli, 2010; Grefenstette and Sadrzadeh, 2011) should provide further benefits.

The state of the art is a supervised method based on Recurrent Convolutional Neural Networks (Kalchbrenner and Blunsom, 2013). This method learns both the sentence model and the discourse model from the same training corpus, making it hard to understand how much of the contribution comes from the inclusion of distributional word meaning, and how much from learning patterns specific to the corpus at hand. Here, in contrast, we use an external unlabeled resource to obtain a model of word meaning, composing words to obtain representations for utterances, and rely on training data only for discourse learning for the tagging task itself.

We proceed as follows. First, we discuss related work by introducing distributional semantics and describe common approaches for dialogue act tagging in Section 2. Section 3 proposes several models for utterance representation based on the bag of words approach and word vector composition. We describe the experiment and discuss the result in Section 4. Finally, Section 5 concludes the work.

## 2 Related work

**Distributional semantics** The aim of natural language semantics is to provide logical representations of meaning for information in textual form. Distributional semantics is based on the idea that "You shall know a word by the company it keeps" (Firth, 1957) – in other words, the meaning of a word is related to the contexts it appears in. Following this idea, word meaning can be represented as a vector where its dimensions correspond to the usage contexts, usually other words observed to co-occur, and the values are the co-occurrence frequencies. Such a meaning representation is easy to build from raw data and does not need rich annotation.

Methods based on this distributional hypothesis have recently been applied to many tasks, but mostly at the word level: for instance, word sense disambiguation (Zhitomirsky-Geffet and Dagan, 2009) and lexical substitution (Thater et al., 2010). They exploit the notion of similarity which correlates with the angle between word vectors (Turney et al., 2010). *Compositional* distributional semantics goes beyond the word level and models the meaning of phrases or sentences based on their parts. Mitchell and Lapata (2008) perform composition of word vectors using vector addition and multiplication operations. The limitation of this approach is the operator associativity, which ignores the argument order, and thus word order. As a result, "*John loves Mary*" and "*Mary loves John*" get assigned the same meaning.

To capture word order, various approaches have been proposed. Grefenstette and Sadrzadeh (2011) extend the compositional approach by using non-associative linear algebra operators as proposed in the theoretical work of (Coecke et al., 2010). Socher et al. (2012) present a recursive technique to build compositional meaning of phrases from their constituents, where the nonlinear composition operators are learned by Neural Networks.

**Dialogue act tagging** There are many ways to approach the task of dialogue act tagging (Stolcke et al., 2000). The most successful approaches combine *intra*-utterance features, such as the (sequences of) words and intonational contours used, together with *inter*-utterance features, such as the sequence of utterance tags being used previously. To capture both of these aspects, sequence models such as Hidden Markov Models are widely used (Stolcke et al., 2000; Surendran and Levow, 2006). The sequence of words is an observable variable, while the sequence of dialogue act tags is a hidden variable.

However, some approaches have shown competitive results without exploiting features of inter-utterance context. Webb et al. (2005) concentrate only on features found inside an utterance, identifying ngrams that correlate strongly with particular utterance tags, and propose a statistical model for prediction which produces close to the state of the art results.

The current state of the art (Kalchbrenner and Blunsom, 2013) uses Recurrent Convolutional Neural Networks to achieve high accuracy. This model includes information about word identity, intra-utterance word sequence, and inter-utterance tag sequence, by using a vector space model of words with a compositional approach. The words vectors are not based on distributional frequencies in this case, however, but on randomly initialised vectors, with the model trained on a specific corpus. This raises several questions: what is the contribution of word sequence and/or utterance (tag) sequence; and might further gains be made by exploiting the distributional hypothesis?

As our baseline, we start with an approach which uses only word information, and excludes word sequence, tag sequence and word distributions. Serafin et al. (2003) use Latent Semantic Analysis for dialogue act tagging: utterances are represented using a bag-of-words representation in a word-document matrix. The rows in the matrix correspond to words, the columns correspond to documents and each cell in the matrix contains the number of times a word occurs in a document. Singular Value Decomposition (SVD) is then applied to reduce the number of rows in the matrix, with the number of components in the reduced space set to 50. To predict the tag of an unseen utterance, the utterance vector is mapped to the reduced space and the tag of the closest neighbor is assigned to it (using cosine similarity as a similarity measure). The reported accuracy on the Spanish Call Home corpus for predicting 37 different utterance tags is 65.36%.

## 3 Utterance models

In this paper, we investigate the extent to which distributional representations, word order information, and utterance order information can improve this basic model, by choosing different ways to represent an utterance in a vector space. We design three basic models. The first model is based directly on the bag-of-words model which serves as the baseline in our experiment, following (Serafin et al., 2003); and extends this to investigate the effect of word order information by moving from word unigrams to bigrams. The second model investigates distributional information, by calculating word vector representations from a general corpus, and obtaining utterance representations by composing the word vectors using simple operators. The third model extends this idea to investigate the role of utterance order information, by including the information about the previous utterance.

**Bag of words** The first model represents an utterance as a vector where each component corresponds to a word. The values of vector components are the number of times the corresponding words occured in the utterance. The model is similar to (Serafin et al., 2003), but the matrix is transposed. We refer to it as *bag of unigrams* in Table 1.

However, this bag of words approach does not preserve any word order information. As it has been said previously, for the dialogue act tagging word order may be crucial. Consider these utterances:

- *John, are there cookies*
- *John, there are cookies*

One of the utterances is a question (or request) while the other is a statement. However, the bag of words model will extract the same vector representation for both.

To overcome this problem we also represent an utterance as a *bag of bigrams*. When bigrams are used in place of single words, the utterance representation will differ. The question contains the bigram "*are there*", while the statement contains the bigram "*there are*".

**Simple composition** Our second model exploits the distributional hypothesis, by representing words not as atomic types (i.e. individual dimensions in the utterance matrix, as above), but as vectors encoding their observed co-occurrence distributions. We estimate these from a large corpus of general written English (the Google Books Ngrams corpus – see below).

However, this raises the question of how to compose these word vectors into a single representation for an utterance. Various approaches to compositional vector space modelling have been successfully applied to capture the meaning of a phrase in a range of tasks (Mitchell and Lapata, 2008; Grefenstette and Sadrzadeh, 2011; Socher et al., 2013). In this work, we follow (Mitchell and Lapata, 2008) and apply vector addition and point-wise multiplication to obtain the vector of an utterance from the words it consists of. This has the advantage of simplicity and domain-generality, requiring no sentence grammar (problematic for the non-canonical language in dialogue) or training on a specific corpus to obtain the appropriate compositionality operators or associative model; but has the disadvantage of losing word order information. The corresponding models are referred as *addition* and *multiplication* in Table 1 and Table 2.

**Previous utterance** A conversation is a sequence of utterances, and the tag of an utterance often depends on the previous utterance (e.g. answers tend to follow questions). Hidden Markov Models (Surendran and Levow, 2006; Stolcke et al., 2000) are often used to capture these dependencies; Recurrent Convolutional Neural Networks (Kalchbrenner and Blunsom, 2013) have been used to simultaneously capture the intra-utterance sequence of words and the inter-utterance sequence of dialog tags in a conversation.

In this model, we are interested specifically in the effect of inter-utterance (tag) sequence. We provide *previous addition* and *previous multiplication* models as simple attempts to capture this phenomenon: the vector of an utterance is the concatenation of its vector obtained in the corresponding compositional model (*addition* or *multiplication*) and the vector of the previous utterance.

## 4 Predicting dialogue acts

### 4.1 The resources

This section describes the resources we use to evaluate and compare the proposed models.

**Switchboard corpus** The Switchboard corpus (Godfrey et al., 1992) is a corpus of telephone conversations on selected topics. It consists of about 2500 conversations by 500 speakers from the U.S. The conversations in the corpus are labeled with 42 unique dialogue act tags and split to 1115 train

```
A o    : Okay. /
A qw   : {D So, }
B qy^d: [ [I guess, +
A +    : What kind of experience
         [ do you, + do you ] have,
          then with child care? /
B +    : I think, ] + {F uh, }
         I wonder if that worked. /
```

(a) A conversation with interrupted utterances.

```
A o    : Okay.
A qw   : So What kind of experience
         do you do you have then
         with child care?
B qy^d: I guess I think uh I wonder
         if that worked.
```

(b) A preprocessed conversation.

Figure 1: A example of interrupted utterances from Switchboard and their transformation.

and 19 test conversations (Jurafsky et al., 1997; Stolcke et al., 2000).

In addition to the dialog act tags, utterances interrupted by the other speaker (and thus split into two or more parts) have their continuations marked with a special tag "+". Tag prediction of one part of an interrupted utterance in isolation is a difficult task even for a human; for example, it would not be clear why the utterance *"So,"* should be assigned the tag `qw` (wh-question) in Figure 1a without the second part *"What kind of experience do you have [...]"*. Following (Webb et al., 2005) we preprocess Switchboard by concatenating the parts of an interrupted utterance together, giving the result the tag of the first part and putting it in its place in the conversation sequence. We also remove commas and disfluency markers from the raw text. Figure 1b illustrates the transformation we do as preprocessing.

We split the utterances between training and testing as suggested in (Stolcke et al., 2000).

**Google Books Ngram Corpus** The Google Books Ngram Corpus (Lin et al., 2012) is a collection of n-gram frequencies over books written in 8 languages. The English part of the corpus is based on more than 4.5 million books and contains more than four thousand billion tokens. The resource provides frequencies of n-grams of length 1 to 5. For our experiments we use 5-grams from the English part of the resource.

### 4.2 Word vector spaces

In distributional semantics, the meanings of words are captured by a vector space model based on a word co-occurrence matrix. Each row in the matrix represents a target word, and each column represents a context word; each element in the matrix is the number of times a target word co-occured with a corresponding context word. The frequency counts are typically normalized, or weighted using tf-idf or log-likelihood ratio to obtain better results, see (Mitchell and Lapata, 2008; Agirre et al., 2009) for various approaches. It is also common to apply dimensionality reduction to get higher performance (Dinu and Lapata, 2010; Baroni and Zamparelli, 2010).

As target words we select all the words in our (Switchboard) training split. As context words we choose the 3000 most frequent words in the Google Ngram Corpus, excluding the 100 most frequent. To obtain co-occurrence frequencies from ngrams we sum up the frequency of a 5-gram over the years, treat the word in the middle as a target, and the other words as its contexts.

For normalization, we experiment with a vector space based on raw co-occurrences; a vector space where frequencies are weighted using tf-idf; and another one with the number of dimensions reduced to 1000 using Non-negative Matrix Factorization (NMF) (Hoyer, 2004).

We use the NMF and tf-idf implementations provided by `scikit-learn` version 0.14 (Pedregosa et al., 2011). For tf-idf, the term vectors are $L^2$ normalized. For NMF, NNDSVD initialization (Boutsidis and Gallopoulos, 2008) is used, and the tolerance value for stopping conditions is set to 0.001. The co-occurrence matrix is line-normalized, so the sum of the values in each row is 1 before applying NMF.[1]

### 4.3 Evaluation

To evaluate these possible models we follow (Serafin et al., 2003). Once we have applied a model to extract features from utterances and build a vector space, the dimensionality of the vector space is reduced using SVD to 50 dimensions. Then a k-nearest neighbours (KNN) classifier is trained and used for utterance tag prediction. In contrast to (Serafin et al., 2003), we use Euclidean distance as a distance metric and choose the most

[1]The co-occurrence matrix and the information about the software used in the experiment are available at http://www.eecs.qmul.ac.uk/~dm303/cvsc14.html

| Method | Accuracy |
|---|---|
| (Kalchbrenner and Blunsom, 2013) | **0.739** |
| (Webb et al., 2005) | 0.719 |
| (Stolcke et al., 2000) | 0.710 |
| (Serafin et al., 2003) | *0.654* |
| Bag of unigrams | 0.602 |
| Bag of bigrams | 0.621 |
| Addition | 0.639 |
| Multiplication | 0.572 |
| Previous addition | 0.569 |
| Previous multiplication | 0.497 |

Table 1: Comparison with previous work. Note that (Serafin et al., 2003) do not use Switchboard and therefore their results are not directly comparable to others.

frequent label among the 5 closest neighbors. The SVD and KNN classifier implementations in `scikit-learn` are used.

**Baseline** In our experiments, the bag of unigrams model accuracy of 0.602 is lower than the accuracy of 0.654 reported in (Serafin et al., 2003), see Table 1. The lower performance may be due to the differences between Switchboard and CallHome37 corpora, in particular the tag distribution.[2] In CallHome37, 42.7% of utterances are labeled with the most frequent dialogue act, while the figure in Switchboard is 31.5%; the more even distribution in Switchboard is likely to make overall average accuracy levels lower.

**Word order** As Table 1 shows, the bag of bigrams model improves over unigrams. This confirms that word order provides important information for predicting dialogue act tags.

**Distributional models** Performance of compositional distributional models depends both on compositional operator and weighting. Table 2 demonstrates accuracy of the models. We instantiate 3 vector spaces from Google Ngrams: one space with raw co-occurrence frequencies, a tf-idf weighted space and a reduced space using NMF.

Addition outperforms multiplication in our experiments, although for other tasks multiplication has been shown to perform better (Grefenstette and Sadrzadeh, 2011; Mitchell and Lapata, 2008). Lower multiplication performance here might be

[2]The CallHome37 corpus is not currently available to us.

| | Space | | |
|---|---|---|---|
| Model | Raw | tf-idf | NMF |
| Addition without SVD | 0.592 | | |
| Addition | 0.610 | **0.639** | 0.620 |
| Multiplication | 0.572 | 0.568 | 0.525 |
| Previous addition | | | 0.569 |
| Previous multiplication | | | 0.497 |

Table 2: Accuracy results for different compositional models and vector spaces.

due to the fact that some utterances are rather long (for example, more than 70 tokens), and the resulting vectors get many zero components.

Selection of the optimal weighting method could be crucial for overall model performance. The 3 weighting schemes we use give a broad variety of results; more elaborate weighting and context selection might give higher results.

Figure 2 illustrates dialog tag assignment using addition and the tf-idf weighted vector space. As we do not use any inter-utterance features, the first two statements, which consist only of the word *Okay*, got assigned wrong tags. However, the Wh-question in the conversation got classified as a Yes-No-question, probably because *what* did not influence the classification decision strongly enough and could have been classified correctly using only intra-utterance features. Also, the example shows how important grammatical features are: the verb *think* appears in many different context, and its presence does not indicate a certain type of an utterance.

In addition, we observed that SVD improves classification accuracy. The accuracy of KNN classification without prior dimensionality reduction drops from 0.610 to 0.592 for vector addition on the raw vector space.

**Utterance sequence** To solve the issue of utterances that can be tagged correctly only by considering inter-utterance features, we included previous utterance. However, in our experiment, such inclusion by vector concatenation does not improve tagging accuracy (Table 2). The reason for this could be that after concatenation the dimensionality of the space doubles, and SVD can not handle it properly. We evaluated only dimensionally reduced spaces because of the memory limit.

```
B **   (b) : Okay.
A b^m  (b) : Okay.
B qw   (qy): Well what do you think about the idea of uh kids having to do public
             service work for a year?
B qy   (sd): Do you think it's a <breathing>
A sv   (sv): Well I I think it's a pretty good idea.
A sv   (sd): I think they should either do that or or afford some time to the military
             or or helping elderly people.
B aa   (aa): Yes
B aa   (b) : yes
B %    (%) : def
A sv   (sv): I I you know I think that we have a bunch of elderly folks in the country
             that could use some help
```

Figure 2: The beginning of the conversation 2151 from the test split of Switchboard. In brackets the tags predicted using vector addition as a composition method on the tf-idf space are given. We mark `fo_o_fw_"_by_bc` as `**`.

**Summary** Our accuracy is lower compared to other work. Webb et al. (2005)'s method, based only on intra-utterance lexical features, but incorporating longer ngram sequences and feature selection, yields accuracy of 0.719. Advanced treatment of both utterance and discourse level features yields accuracy of 0.739 (Kalchbrenner and Blunsom, 2013). However, our experiments allow us to evaluate the contribution of various kinds of information: vector spaces based on word bigrams and on co-occurrence distributions both outperformed the bag of words approach; but incorporation of previous utterance information did not.

## 5 Conclusions and future work

In this work we evaluated the contribution of word and utterance sequence, and of distributional information using simple compositional vector space models, for dialogue act tagging. Our experiments show that information about intra-utterance word order (ngrams), and information about word co-occurence distributions, outperforms the bag of words models, although not competitive with the state of the art given the simplistic compositional approach used here. Information about utterance tag sequence, on the other hand, did not.

The usage of an external, large scale resource (here, the Google Ngram Corpus) to model word senses improves the tagging accuracy in comparison to the bag of word model, suggesting that the dialogue act tag of an utterance depends on its semantics.

However, the improvements in performance of the *bag of bigrams* model in comparison to *bag of unigrams*, and the much higher results of Webb et al. (2005)'s intra-utterance approach, suggest that the sequence of words inside an utterance is crucial for the dialogue act tagging task. This suggests that our simplistic approaches to vector composition (addition and multiplication) are likely to be insufficient: more advanced, sequence- or grammar-driven composition, such as categorical composition (Coecke et al., 2010), might improve the tagging accuracy.

In addition, our results show that the performance of distributional models depends on many factors, including compositional operator selection and weighting of the initial co-occurrence matrix. Our work leaves much scope for improvements in these factors, including co-occurrence matrix instantiation. For example, the window size of 2, which we used to obtain co-occurrence counts, is lower than the usual size of 5 (Dinu and Lapata, 2010), or the sentence level (Baroni and Zamparelli, 2010). Word representation in a vector space using neural networks might improve accuracy as well (Mikolov et al., 2013).

Previous approaches to dialogue act tagging have shown utterance/tag sequence to be a useful source of information for improved accuracy (Stolcke et al., 2000). We therefore conclude that the lower accuracy we obtained using models that include information about the previous utterance is due again to our simplistic method of composition (vector concatenation); models which reflect dialogue structure or sequence explicitly are likely to be more suited. Kalchbrenner and Blunsom (2013) give one way in which this can be achieved by learning from a specific corpus, and the question of possible alternatives and more general models remains for future research.

## Acknowledgments

We thank Mehrnoosh Sadrzadeh for her helpful advice and valuable discussion. We would like to thank anonymous reviewers for their effective comments. Milajevs is supported by the EP-SRC project EP/J002607/1. Purver is supported in part by the European Community's Seventh Framework Programme under grant agreement no 611733 (ConCreTe).

## References

Eneko Agirre, Enrique Alfonseca, Keith Hall, Jana Kravalova, Marius Paşca, and Aitor Soroa. 2009. A study on similarity and relatedness using distributional and wordnet-based approaches. In *Proceedings of Human Language Technologies: The 2009 Annual Conference of the North American Chapter of the Association for Computational Linguistics*, pages 19–27. Association for Computational Linguistics.

Marco Baroni and Roberto Zamparelli. 2010. Nouns are vectors, adjectives are matrices: Representing adjective-noun constructions in semantic space. In *Proceedings of the 2010 Conference on Empirical Methods in Natural Language Processing*, pages 1183–1193. Association for Computational Linguistics.

Christos Boutsidis and Efstratios Gallopoulos. 2008. Svd based initialization: A head start for nonnegative matrix factorization. *Pattern Recognition*, 41(4):1350–1362.

Bob Coecke, Mehrnoosh Sadrzadeh, and Stephen Clark. 2010. Mathematical foundations for a compositional distributional model of meaning. *CoRR*, abs/1003.4394.

Mark Core. 1998. Analyzing and predicting patterns of damsl utterance tags. In *Proceedings of the AAAI spring symposium on Applying machine learning to discourse processing*.

G. Dinu and M. Lapata. 2010. Measuring distributional similarity in context. In *Proceedings of the 2010 Conference on Empirical Methods in Natural Language Processing*, pages 1162–1172. Association for Computational Linguistics.

John R. Firth. 1957. A Synopsis of Linguistic Theory, 1930-1955. *Studies in Linguistic Analysis*, pages 1–32.

John J Godfrey, Edward C Holliman, and Jane McDaniel. 1992. Switchboard: Telephone speech corpus for research and development. In *Acoustics, Speech, and Signal Processing, 1992. ICASSP-92., 1992 IEEE International Conference on*, volume 1, pages 517–520. IEEE.

Edward Grefenstette and Mehrnoosh Sadrzadeh. 2011. Experimental support for a categorical compositional distributional model of meaning. In *Proceedings of the Conference on Empirical Methods in Natural Language Processing*, pages 1394–1404. Association for Computational Linguistics.

Patrik O Hoyer. 2004. Non-negative matrix factorization with sparseness constraints. *The Journal of Machine Learning Research*, 5:1457–1469.

Daniel Jurafsky, Elizabeth Shriberg, and Debra Biasca. 1997. Switchboard swbd-damsl shallow-discourse-function annotation coders manual, draft 13. Technical Report 97-02, University of Colorado, Boulder. Institute of Cognitive Science.

Daniel Jurafsky, Elizabeth Shriberg, Barbara Fox, and Traci Curl. 1998. Lexical, prosodic, and syntactic cues for dialog acts. In *Proceedings of the ACL-COLING Workshop on Discourse Relations and Discourse Markers*.

Nal Kalchbrenner and Phil Blunsom. 2013. Recurrent convolutional neural networks for discourse compositionality. In *Proceedings of the Workshop on Continuous Vector Space Models and their Compositionality*, pages 119–126, Sofia, Bulgaria, August. Association for Computational Linguistics.

Yuri Lin, Jean-Baptiste Michel, Erez Lieberman Aiden, Jon Orwant, Will Brockman, and Slav Petrov. 2012. Syntactic annotations for the Google Books ngram corpus. In *Proceedings of the ACL 2012 System Demonstrations*, pages 169–174. Association for Computational Linguistics.

Tomas Mikolov, Kai Chen, Greg Corrado, and Jeffrey Dean. 2013. Efficient estimation of word representations in vector space. *arXiv preprint arXiv:1301.3781*.

Jeff Mitchell and Mirella Lapata. 2008. Vector-based models of semantic composition. In *Proceedings of ACL-08: HLT*, pages 236–244. Association for Computational Linguistics.

F. Pedregosa, G. Varoquaux, A. Gramfort, V. Michel, B. Thirion, O. Grisel, M. Blondel, P. Prettenhofer, R. Weiss, V. Dubourg, J. Vanderplas, A. Passos, D. Cournapeau, M. Brucher, M. Perrot, and E. Duchesnay. 2011. Scikit-learn: Machine learning in Python. *Journal of Machine Learning Research*, 12:2825–2830.

Riccardo Serafin, Barbara Di Eugenio, and Michael Glass. 2003. Latent semantic analysis for dialogue act classification. In *Proceedings of the 2003 Conference of the North American Chapter of the Association for Computational Linguistics on Human Language Technology: companion volume of the Proceedings of HLT-NAACL 2003–short papers-Volume 2*, pages 94–96. Association for Computational Linguistics.

Richard Socher, Brody Huval, Christopher D Manning, and Andrew Y Ng. 2012. Semantic compositionality through recursive matrix-vector spaces. In *Proceedings of the 2012 Joint Conference on Empirical Methods in Natural Language Processing and Computational Natural Language Learning*, pages 1201–1211. Association for Computational Linguistics.

Richard Socher, John Bauer, Christopher D Manning, and Andrew Y Ng. 2013. Parsing with compositional vector grammars. In *In Proceedings of the ACL conference*. Citeseer.

Andreas Stolcke, Klaus Ries, Noah Coccaro, Elizabeth Shriberg, Rebecca Bates, Daniel Jurafsky, Paul Taylor, Carol Van Ess-Dykema, Rachel Martin, and Marie Meteer. 2000. Dialogue act modeling for automatic tagging and recognition of conversational speech. *Computational Linguistics*, 26(3):339–373.

Dinoj Surendran and Gina-Anne Levow. 2006. Dialog act tagging with support vector machines and hidden markov models. In *INTERSPEECH*.

Stefan Thater, Hagen Fürstenau, and Manfred Pinkal. 2010. Contextualizing semantic representations using syntactically enriched vector models. In *Proceedings of the 48th Annual Meeting of the Association for Computational Linguistics*, ACL '10, pages 948–957, Stroudsburg, PA, USA. Association for Computational Linguistics.

Peter D Turney, Patrick Pantel, et al. 2010. From frequency to meaning: Vector space models of semantics. *Journal of artificial intelligence research*, 37(1):141–188.

Nick Webb, Mark Hepple, and Yorick Wilks. 2005. Dialogue act classification based on intra-utterance features. In *Proceedings of the AAAI Workshop on Spoken Language Understanding*. Citeseer.

M. Zhitomirsky-Geffet and I. Dagan. 2009. Bootstrapping distributional feature vector quality. *Computational Linguistics*, 35(3):435–461.

# Author Index